The Urbanization of the Earth

THE URBANIZATION OF THE EARTH

by Jorge Arango

Introduction by José Luis Sert

BEACON PRESS   BOSTON

Copyright © 1970 by Jorge Arango
Library of Congress catalog card number: 78–119674
International Standard Book Number: 0–8070–0882–6
Beacon Press books are published under the auspices
of the Unitarian Universalist Association
Published simultaneously in Canada by Saunders of Toronto, Ltd.
Printed in the United States of America

Contents

The earth is suffering a traumatic adaptation from the agricultural era man is leaving to the scientific and industrial one he is entering. As with the founding of man's first settlements and the advent of farming, the process is irreversible. People did not go back to marauding and hunting, and people will not go back to the farms or small and isolated towns where life even now continues to be quiet and unhurried. Science and industrialization are creating a new kind of society. To those still committed to the agricultural way of life, it seems slavery—inhuman, regimented, time-conscious, precision-obsessed. Nevertheless, this new kind of society is taking over the earth. It will probably complete its task in one percent of the time it took agriculture to build the civilization man is now leaving.

About fifteen thousand years have gone by since man settled down and built cities. To wandering hunters for whom life was adventure, settling down and working the land must have seemed unbearably dull. Repetitious daily tasks, security, domesticity—what a bore! Nevertheless, in a period equaling only one percent of man's history, those commercial and agricultural people took over the earth and left the hunters wandering on very reduced ground: the tundra, the desert, and a few humid jungles.

For over one hundred centuries people used the city mainly for trade and protection; only about one out of ten lived there. The rest lived on the land. Life was unhurried, interrupted only by wars, which satisfied the urge for adventure man inherited from his hunter ancestors. But in the last hundred years this condition changed. Mendel's discovery of the principles of heredity in the mid-nineteenth century resulted in scientific cross-breeding and dramatic improvement in the yields of agriculture. Pasteur's demonstration of the principle of infection brought about a revolution in the prevention and cure of diseases in plants, animals, and men. With more food and better health the number of people on earth trebled in barely a century. During this same time the Industrial Revolution occurred, and it took fewer hands to operate machines that made more and better goods. Production shifted from the fields to the cities. These once-peaceful places of residence and exchange of goods now became the busy principal producers. At the same time that the small population of the earth grew large, a gigantic migration toward the urban areas began. Soon cities became crowded workshops in which industry manufactured goods in quantities never heard or dreamed of before. Consumption stimulated appetite for still more goods, not for a few but for everybody. Social and economic ideas sprouted and political problems proliferated.

These are the main facts. But there are secondary developments that further complicate the present urban situation. For example, as cities became crowded they expanded, and as they expanded they required means of transportation. Industry supplied transportation machines that made the cities even more crowded and forced even further expansion. The metabolism of industry is high. Its digestive process leaves a residue which pollutes the air and water from which men, animals, and plants live.

The world today is made up of societies in different stages, all evolving toward industrialization. Most of them are poor by the new industrial standards, and most have rapidly expanding populations that are on the move toward cities struggling to keep up with a tidal wave of humanity and machines. With modern means of communication, societies in one stage of evolution influence societies in another, creating a certain amount of healthy stimulation but simultaneously causing a great deal of confusion.

Wars still exist but the adventurousness has disappeared. Industry made war rely on production efficiency and meticulous planning rather than individual initiative, courage, and flair. Now science has put a final period to the fun of war. The wars of the first half of the twentieth century have not been entirely negative. Through them man became immersed in the scientific and industrial age.

But man has still to use fully this new scientific and industrial power to build in peacetime. It has been tested only in wars or in rebuilding after them. Until recently it took centuries and many generations for countries to recuperate from the devastation of wars. Even in the United States it took the South one hundred years. But in our time, in spite of the fact that the power of destruction of modern warfare is a thousand times greater, industrial countries such as Germany and Japan have not only rebuilt themselves but have reached new heights of prosperity in a fraction of a century.

In those areas in which science and industry have been applied for peaceful purposes, they have produced immediate and gigantic results which have either created equally gigantic problems or simply gone to waste, not because the tools or intentions were wrong but because man has yet to learn to handle his new power. Thus improvements in health and the control of infectious diseases have not made man better or life easier; they have merely created overpopulation. And most of the colossal power of electronic communication is wasted on childish entertainment. Meanwhile the cities, after years of prosperity during the blossoming of the agricultural era, are collapsing under the impetus of industrialization. And man, afraid of his own new power and lost in his new industrial environment, stumbles and looks for support to the familiar forms which, day by day, are disappearing with an era that is ending and will never return.

Much of what has been recently written about our environment in general and about cities in particular is limited to the possible changes within an existing narrow framework imposed by the conditions prevailing today. Legal restraints, political barriers, accepted routine methods of financing, and outmoded zoning and building codes paralyzed any real changes.

The physical forms of things around us are the natural expression of the form-giving process. To "design" is to limit, to define. What has and is being designed is a faithful expression of the goals and values of contemporary society.

If the development of the environment is understood as a process of limitless profit for the few, of uncontrolled speculation, the perfect formulas have already been found. If profits mean quick returns on investments, no planning is needed—planning is an obstacle in the free-for-all, laissez-faire competitive market. But there is an increasing awareness and a pressing demand today for a radical change in attitude toward the environment. Ecology is rapidly becoming a meaningful word to great numbers of people, especially young people. The younger generation is developing an entirely new set of values that together with the awareness of the decay of our natural environment and our communities is becoming a worldwide protest movement capable of transforming the human habitat.

There is a need for books dealing with generalities, taking a worldwide view of urban conditions as nationalities and frontiers are steadily eroded by revolutionary changes in communications and transportation. Much energy is being put into analyzing the prevailing conditions in our cities. We have all the facts, but we lack courage and new thinking. In spite of the new means and tools at our disposal, we only propose halfway solutions to conditions that require radical changes.

The Urbanization of the Earth takes a broad view of existing conditions in cities and the causes of decay. It emphasizes the physical aspects of the environment, which is natural considering the author is an architect. The worldwide view that may seem too ambitious is appropriate. Our young people travel more and faster than any previous generation. The global picture and the magnitude of various problems do not discourage them. Many are generalists, and generalists are badly needed. Previous generations have specialized in preparing specialists. The world needs both, working in teams.

The complexity of existing conditions and the variety of factors that have caused the decay of our environment cannot be fully covered in a book of this type. It would require many specialists of many professions. Several general statements may be called one-sided, and other views expressed here, utopian. Experts in past years have considered "utopian" the realities of today—pragmatism has been more fashionable, utopias are not known to produce quick returns. But the younger generations are increasingly aware that many so-called "utopias" may materialize during their life spans. They are beginning to measure what is needed to salvage and transform what is worthwhile in our environment, urban or rural. Faith is needed to get things changed. While a few years ago it was generally believed that such changes were impossible, there is a new vision today encouraged by the materialization of "utopias."

Some chapters could be added to this book, envisioning the consequences of radical changes in the accepted values of today. In the chapters, "U.S.A., the Coast-to-Coast Town," Arango makes some devastating statements that are only too true. These brilliant generalizations keep the tone of the book responsive to its title.

This country has seen two generations of timid planners. They are proud to be called "realistic" when this is too often a disguise for lack of imagination and courage to envision the changes our times call for. In their approach obstacles in the way of change are the first things to consider. Theirs is an obstacle race, without courage to jump over barriers or demolish them—the majority are allergic to design. We may be getting out of this jungle, nonetheless. During my years of teaching at the Harvard Graduate School of Design I have known many young people who took a somewhat less respectful attitude toward established values, and I am hopeful they will have the imaginative and courageous views our changing times require.

I do not share Arango's opposition to zoning, although I certainly agree that zoning as practiced today is more hindrance than help. Arango is also too willing to accept low density patterns rather than compactness and planned density, for which I stand. He may be too confident that the large-scale measures outlined in his plans are acceptable to the existing systems.

It is right to approach the theme of urbanization in a worldwide picture, emphasizing the things all people have in common, which bring them together, when so many books deal with the small differences that drive men apart.

The Urbanization of the Earth outlines with clarity and conciseness the ups and downs of cities, past and present. It should help the layman understand the magnitude and causes of the decay of the human environment and the pressing need for a revision of values that will help open new horizons. Jorge Arango comes from a Latin country where marathon talk-ins have been taking place in the cafés for years, and he has become a well-trained debater. The book is opinionated, as it should be; but it is also witty and agreeable to read—a rare virtue in books dealing with this subject.

—José Luis Sert

The Urbanization of the Earth

With statistics it has been possible to discover that man, seen in enough quantity and through a long enough period of time, behaves in patterns that can be studied scientifically. Statistics are very new to us. We are still as fascinated with them as a child with a pair of binoculars: an average man walks a hundred miles in a year and in his lifetime would be able to walk around the earth. If anybody remembered that in the morning, he would stay in bed. If he remembered that every year he filters 15,000 gallons of liquid through his kidneys, more reason to stay in bed. Obviously he would not have time or energy for anything else.

Population is one of the favorite subjects for statistics. Like the child with binoculars we can create very interesting effects, depending on whether we look through one end of the lens or the other.

The nineteenth century, having developed the first industrial machines and created the basis of the scientific approach to human behavior, made the mistake of mixing the two together, so that life was conceived of in terms of a machine. If considered in those terms, man's geometrical population growth would eventually make him cover every inch of the earth. A similar geometrical growth rate affects birds, rats, and bacteria so that, if this kind of thinking is carried to its logical extreme, we would expect the world to be soon cov-

"The Dream," by Henri Rousseau. Courtesy of the Museum of Modern Art, New York.

ered by a soft lining several feet deep made up of one living thing feeding on another. For example, *Stilonychia*, one of the infusoria, reproduces itself by segmentation five times a day. If it could keep up this pace for one month, a single plant would produce a total of two to the one hundred fiftieth power, which is a million times the volume of the sun.

Today we know that the ecology of nature is not as simple as a nineteenth-century machine, that life is very complicated, and does not begin or end at the cell, the organ, the animal, the society of animals, or the universe. Life is a function of time, and time is still beyond our comprehension. Life exists and behaves in relation to and as a function of everything else that existed, is existing, and will exist. We know that our behavior is subject to what happened billions of years ago in other worlds which we are receiving today as energy that has been traveling through space for those many years. Life is a function of the past but also of the present and future.

There is nothing more exciting than to observe a group of plants of various sizes struggling to perform. Most plants keep a distance from one another. A tree never grows branches into its neighbor if it can avoid doing so. Plants like the sun, but at the same time like to be in a comfortable shade. They like to have maximum space of their own, but at the same time to be together. This interrelation makes plants subordinate their growth to the growth of others. In varieties which have only a few large leaves, the production of a new leaf is an important event which takes a great deal of time and vitality. It is a large investment, worthwhile only if it produces large benefits in light-catching. Only when conditions seem favorable is a decision made. All the plant's resources are then thrown into building the leaf quickly and successfully.

Each plant in a group has similar problems. The result is

the location of each leaf in the most advantageous position, not only for the plant, but for the group. A prediction of timing, size, and location for each leaf in relation to the others would constitute billions of equations changing continuously in time. Each leaf is a unit. Each plant is a unit and each group of plants is a unit also. Here, as everywhere, nature plays a symphony in time and space, in which each instrument performs with the right intensity at the right moment.

We are products of the evolution of nature and carry in ourselves the essence of nature. We are made out of gravity and water, of sunlight and time. We communicate with nature through millions of channels; we are only conscious of the few that affect our brain and are useful for our immediate behavior.

Only in great emergencies does nature solve problems with wholesale death, yet many billions of seeds are wasted each season. Only when the chances are good does nature embark on the enterprise of life. But when there is a chance of extinction, nature can battle back with wholesale birth or growth. This is the case after great calamities when the birth rate or growth increases rapidly. It is true, for instance, of man's birth rate after wars, and vegetable growth after a hurricane, fire or flood. When conditions of survival are so grave that no alternative is left, life can also remain dormant for a long time before giving up completely.

The tropics is a place where life seems to thrive. There is probably more life per square inch in the Amazon than per square mile in the Antarctic. That crowd makes competition arduous and causes all types of life to grow with a short, fast turnover. In the tropical countries, man's birth rate is high, forty to fifty-five per thousand, compared to Europe where the birth rate is lower than twenty per thousand. Life is short:

forty-five years life expectancy, compared to sixty-eight years
for Europe and seventy-two years for the United States.

It is true for the world as a whole that as general standards
of living rise, health conditions improve, life expectancy increases, infants' chances of survival are greater, and birth rate
diminishes. A good example is Japan, a country that has improved its standard of living very rapidly since the end of
World War II.

POPULATION OF JAPAN (per 1,000)

Year	Birth Rate	Death Rate	Rate of Natural Increase
1933–37	30.8	17.4	13.4
1945	24.2	27.0	—2.8
1947	34.3	14.6	19.7
1949	33.0	11.6	21.4
1951	25.5	9.9	15.6
1953	21.5	8.8	12.7
1955	19.3	7.8	11.5
1957	17.3	8.3	9.0
1959	17.6	7.5	10.1
1961	16.9	7.4	9.5

Better living conditions bring lower birth rates, even without the use of the pill and other contraceptives. Birth rates
are diminishing in Western Europe.

Year	1890	1900	1913	1930	1939	1947	1955	1960
Births per Thousand	33	29	26	21	19	21	18	18

There is no clear explanation for this natural reduction of the
birth rate, though the subject is at present under investigation. Some scientists have considered even the kind of food;
better-fed people tend to eat more protein.

	Birth Rates per 1,000	Daily Animal Protein Consumption
Formosa	45.6	4.7
Malaysia	39.7	7.5
India	33.0	8.7
Japan	27.0	9.7
Yugoslavia	25.9	11.2
Greece	23.5	15.2
Italy	23.4	15.2
Bulgaria	22.2	16.8
Germany	30.0	37.3
Ireland	19.1	46.7
Denmark	18.1	56.1
Australia	18.0	59.9
United States	17.9	61.4
Sweden	15.0	62.6

This kind of statistic, although interesting, should be taken with a grain of salt, since automobile consumption would probably show a similar ratio. A more likely explanation is the general standard of living and level of education. For the sophisticated urban intellectual, sex is thought of as an adult lollipop. Simple rural people organize their societies around the care of children, while sophisticated societies tend to rely on institutional education. Farmers' children are easy to feed and care for, and soon help in the work of the farm; people living in large urban concentrations consider children a luxury, expensive to keep and an impediment to their freedom. And of course in the large industrial city and especially for the higher income groups, there are all kinds of entertainment to occupy leisure time.

Women in the agricultural regions of the world have, as an average, 50 percent more children than women in urban areas. Even in the industrialized countries the difference between urban and rural populations is striking. In the United

States, for instance, the difference is 32 percent, and in France 25 percent.

The present trend is toward a very fast population increase in the agricultural countries and in those segments of the industrialized countries in which the standard of living is low, especially in rural areas. In most of the industrialized and urbanized societies, birth rates are declining, and with the advent of modern contraceptives, declining fast. On the other hand, the present upsurge is so great that before world population stabilizes it is going to double several times. Population doubled from the year 1 to the year 1650 and the world then had about 500 million people. It doubled again in 180 years, again in one hundred years, and it will probably double again in the following fifty, making a world population of four billion by the year 1980.

There is a direct relationship between population and food, and in that sense, Malthus was correct and men are not different from bacteria, fungi, lice, or mice. But the relation is not a simple one. As goods increase and health improves, the population grows, but, as men become better fed, healthier and educated, the birth rate diminishes. Human wisdom today may be scarce; food should not be. In fact, people today are eating better than ever. Standards of living are improving at a faster rate than population growth, and in that sense Malthus was very wrong. The question is whether the more advanced countries, by supplying food and health facilities to some of the rural backward areas of the world without controlling population expansion, are not really lowering their standard of living by stimulating birth rates.

If food throughout the world were produced with the efficiency achieved today in the United States, the excess would bury us all. And the United States is not growing food with the efficiency it could; it stockpiles a huge surplus in spite of exporting large quantities and granting government subsidies purposely to curb production. Agricultural productivity in the United States has not doubled in the last forty years, as the country's population has—it has increased tenfold. Many experts believe it could still be doubled again with even fewer people on the farm: only five percent of the population are today engaged exclusively in farming. In Europe as a whole, farm population is still close to 40 percent, although stimulated by the Common Market, people are rapidly changing occupations from rural to industrial and migrating from one country to another. Then South America will increase agricultural productivity, then Asia, and later on, Africa. Soon the deserts will be made to produce. More food could be grown on hydroponic farms using city wastes than all of the food that could be grown efficiently on arable land. The manufacture of food directly from chemicals extracted from large sources like the air and sea is not far away either.

But the enlargement of the food cornucopia today does not come from better farming alone. Food is being used more efficiently; nutritional value is being added; canning, freezing, and drying make food last, facilitate its distribution, and drastically reduce waste. At the present time the advanced industrial countries are using food that would have been discarded yesterday, and in many cases these foods make up more than half the total consumption in those countries.

The worried ones can rest their fears. They will not be hungry unless, in their terror that subsistence may be taken from them, they cause the calamities that will leave people with nothing—if there are people left. It is true that two-thirds of the world is not eating enough or well enough. But, remarkably, if India could produce as much rice per capita as

Italy does today, its minimum subsistence problems would be solved.

Malthus was wrong in assuming that hunger was unavoidable, and that population would increase faster than man's means of subsistence. But his fears were not unfounded. Famine has been known since the beginning of history. One of the first was recorded in the Bible, predicted by Joseph as an interpretation of Pharaoh's dream. In more recent history and among closer neighbors, in the century 900–1000 A.D., France had forty-eight recorded famines. In 1770, at least 160,000 people died of hunger in Russia, Bohemia, and Poland, and 120,000 in France. In the year 1877, nine million Chinese and five million in Southern India died in famines. But the worst famines are not recorded. They happened at the beginning of man's history, when scarcity was the normal condition.

The first great increase in man's food supply and consequently in population was produced by the use of weapons to hunt large animals. After all, a buffalo makes up for a lot of berries or lizards. Domestication of animals and agriculture came next, and population increased more quickly. It was possible then to grow crops and have food on a permanent basis. If at one time there was a chance of finding a large prey in one hundred acres, now it was possible to domesticate more than ten similar animals and many smaller ones in the same space. The surplus of labor must have been terrible, since now a few women could take care of the whole operation. Men then decided to spend their time building temples and fortresses, inventing geometry, and trying to figure out what man's existence was about.

At the beginning man relied on his own energy. Later, he began to utilize the energy of the horse, ox, and camel for his own purposes. Then, a short circuit was invented. Instead of letting vegetables, minerals, and water go through the long process of life to create the energy that the horse, ox, or camel could provide, man found a way of making direct use of the energy in nature's air, water, or mineral, first in simple mechanisms like a wind or water mill, later in the cannon which, through an explosion, used the energy latent in minerals. Once the principle was used successfully, development came fast. In a crescendo of inventiveness, steam, electric power, and in recent years, the power of the atom were made available for man's use. By now the sources of energy seem practically inexhaustible.

Not all men developed simultaneously. Some still roam the jungles, the prairies, the deserts, the ice, and the sea in search of prey. The great majority still work the earth and derive their subsistence from agriculture. Only a few societies have reached the industrial and scientific stage.

In 1830, the year the first railroad was inaugurated in the United States, the world reached a population of one billion of which ten percent was urban, mostly living in small towns. Today, only 140 years later, the world has a population 3.5 times larger, 3.5 billion, and the proportion living in cities of over 100,000 people is three times greater. Twelve percent of the earth's population now lives in 141 metropolitan areas of over one million inhabitants. In the nonindustrialized countries, there are today ten to fifteen times the number of city dwellers there were in 1830. In the United States that proportion is 100 to 1.

Machines have taught man a great deal about cause and effect; and mass production, a great deal about organization of ideas in logical sequence. Mass consumption has illuminated his conception of unity within plurality. With the help of statistics man has been able to recognize facts; previously he could only sense tendencies. By now he has learned to plan not only in space but in time.

From the discovery of agriculture to our day, a great distance has been covered in very few years. The population of the world is in a gigantic flow toward urbanization. As people get together and communications improve, the result is not only better utilization of materials and labor, but better utilization of the brain.

Man's life expectancy is also longer because of better food and improved health care. In his extended lifetime he can learn more and utilize his knowledge and experience for a longer period. Three and even four generations live at the same time. The cumulative experience of man has consequently tripled. Furthermore, man has invented computers which multiply that experience millions of times in seconds. Automation has made its entrance. There is no question that in the very near future large numbers of men will have more, produced in less time, by fewer people. There will be an enormous surplus of labor. A similar situation occurred long ago when men discovered agriculture and the domestication of animals. The result was our present civilization.

AN ENVIRONMENT IN SEARCH OF AN ENVIRONMENT

Primitive germs of life float in media from which they do not differ in temperature or chemical composition. Man's history is only a small part of life's three billion years of evolution and search for independence from surrounding media through the creation of its own environment.

Man is the most perfect and complex mechanism nature has yet produced. He carries his own artificial temperature, pressure, and chemical media, and looks at the world from a well-protected cockpit, the head. Man's primitive societies also "floated" in the natural media. As urbanization increased, societies lived in a more and more artificial medium of their own. Today, in the cities of the industrialized countries, man lives in a mostly man-made environment extending from the hospital room where he is born (into artificial light, air composition, and controlled temperature), to the machine-made coffin in which he is buried.

Man himself is an environment, designed by evolution, in which innumerable conglomerations of infinitesimal societies exist and perform in ideal physical conditions. Man is now in the process of creating an artificial physical environment for his own society of men. The development of the human body was a slow trial-and-error process that took billions of years. The development of the man-made physical environment is very recent. The human brain has made progress possible at a speed nature never knew before. Human beings are leaving the natural surroundings in which they have lived for at least a million years, and in a gigantic and sudden historical change will soon complete the urbanization of the earth as the first step in the creation of an artificial environment for their societies. The design of this environment constitutes the most important task man has ever attempted.

As far as we know, life appeared for the first time in the ocean or some quiet lake three or four billion years ago, in a world in which the atmosphere was saturated with water and gases at high temperatures. Proteins and primitive enzymes began to appear as the result of a long process of chemical evolution and formed diminutive systems of molecules enclosed in membranes corresponding to a primitive organization and reminiscent of the present cell. And then, somehow, with the right temperature, pressure, light, and chemical elements, one or many of these, at one instant or many times, and for a long time, created that strange phenomenon called life by which a system is self-maintained and produces others similar to itself.

At some time in the process of the physical evolution of the earth, the temperature of the surface began to fall, the water in the atmosphere to condense, and certain chemical compounds became scarce. Life, to be preserved, had to adapt to new conditions. The primitive elements of life began organizing into primitive infinitesimal systems in an effort to survive. Cells began grouping into primitive societies in which individuals did specialized simple work. At the beginning those cells were not so specialized as to be unable to perform other functions. Later on, specialization became less flexible. These primitive, tiny societies, contained in a sac that separated them from the surrounding media, became the most primitive organisms. As organisms became abundant and life

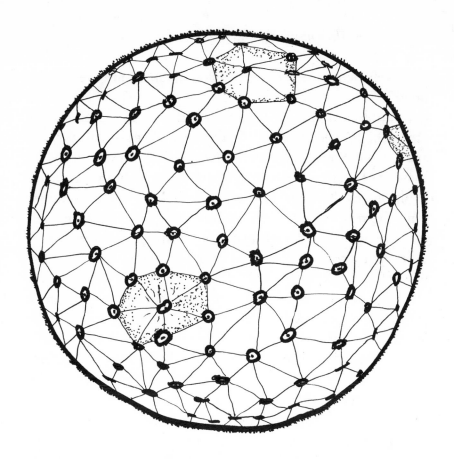

Colony of free living one-cell *volvox* with groups of specialized cells which have taken sexual roles.

more efficient, competition made adaptation even more urgent.

Multiplication by subdivision was the original process. The organism divided itself in two and each one eventually in two and so on. Sometime, somewhere, in its search for better chances of adaptation, nature discovered death and dual sex. With death, there was a chance for a new start, an almost complete renewal from one generation to the next. With dual sex, the chances of faster adaptation increased in a geometrical proportion as desirable qualities became part of the selection of a mate.

Organization of life inside the membrane became more and more complicated, as nature found that life could not be left to the chance of sudden changes in the environment. Too many adaptations could be expensive, wasteful, and hazardous. A race began for more complicated mechanisms that could survive inside their containers, in relatively unsuitable conditions, first, for short periods of time, as when ponds dry during the summer and some fish survive with the use of special water-filled bags of their own, and then for longer periods as species began to appear with a complete survival kit for permanent use.

After many millions of years of a slow searching process, nature developed two very important things, important at least to us, for without them, we would have never known that anything had existed. The first was the brain. The brain was important, for it allowed animals to store information and relay it at different times. The brain also combined information and so the animal acquired experience. The animal could then act before events actually happened, on the basis of circumstances that checked with past events. The other key development was the appearance of the mammal.

Instinct was an accumulation of often outdated experiences. The mammal parents were able to teach the young up-to-date information based on recent experiences. But what was probably most significant in the advent of the mammal was the birth of society. (Insects had societies millions of years before, but insects and mammals are so far separated in their history that they are in fact two different worlds.)

Mother and her newborn became the elements of society. Later on, nature developed love, a force that kept the males around for the period of time in which the females were incapacitated. Social organization progressed as more than one animal family grouped together around a strong and wise male. The exchange of experiences in the newly made societies increased in astronomical proportion. Brain and societies combined set the stage for the appearance of man.

Man arrived at the end of a long three billion years of evolution prepared to survive practically anywhere in the earth's environment. He carries his own water, chemical medium, and food reserves, and maintains an intricate system of pressures and temperatures in different parts of his body. In fact, he is a physical-chemical walking universe in which an incredibly complicated system of societies has achieved harmony and unity, and in which that unity not only acts for its own preservation, but has achieved consciousness of its own existence; it has created a personality. Those innumerable individuals organized in innumerable complicated societies have created their own god.

Man did not reach this stage alone. Other animals arrived at the same time and with almost the same quality of perfection. Like them, man wandered over the earth living on nature's meager subsistence, suffering from hunger and disease. Always adapting to new conditions, he moved over the continents, continually displaced, and ravaged by disease, climate, other animals, and other men.

Quite recently, less than one million years ago, something very important took place. What had happened in nature back at the dawn of life occurred in man: adaptation to the environment was too hard; man, very slowly at the beginning, started to modify the environment to suit himself, as an easier and better system of survival. He did this first in a very primitive way, by changing the shape of a few pieces of flint to make weapons or tools and, fifteen thousand years ago, by domesticating animals and starting agriculture. From that point on, the history of civilization acquired momentum. Mining, fabrication, and commerce eventually brought man to the present industrial and scientific age.

Man began his existence already a social being. It can be guessed that his primitive societies were similar to those of today's nomadic hunting tribes. A group's size was roughly determined by the size of its territory, that is, the space it controlled and within which it searched for food. The size of the group also depended on its ability to defend a large or small territory. The internal social organization at this primitive level probably included a head and a hierarchy of privileges and authority. Monogamy as we know it did not exist, but mating was restricted to the group. Under certain conditions these primitive societies accepted individuals that wandered from one group to the other.

Self-preservation was the original reason for the grouping of infinitesimal elements of life into diminutive primitive organisms contained in a protective membrane. Similarly, when men discovered agriculture and settled in organized groups they protected their settlements by building on sites of difficult access or by providing a protective wall around their huts and possessions. There the city was born.

Most cities of the ancient past were fortresses either built on places of difficult access or surrounded by a wall, or both. For as soon as men had grain and furs in storage to last through the winter, marauding tribes became a menace. Compounds in which grain, animal products, and valuables were stored were the most primitive urban settlements.

Some cities were founded in such safe locations that access was difficult not only for the enemy, but also for a friend. These have survived only as interesting tourist attractions. Some others remained handicapped by locations on high plateaus or on islands where communications are difficult. Some, situated on promontories, at the confluence of rivers or on peninsulas, have found these defense advantages to be great assets in the modern world, as often such locations lend themselves to industry and port facilities.

Each city had its own territory from which to draw and each city defended that territory. Only the city that could draw from a large and rich area became important. Many cities prospered in rich valleys only to shrivel when over-cultivation wore out the soil. Rivers changed courses and left prosperous cities dying in the desert. Large cities thrived, drawing from large rich territories, and later decayed when those territories were lost in battle. As empires were recovered, cities were built on the ruins of the previous ones destroyed by the enemy. Some cities in the Middle East have the ruins of five other cities beneath them. Some cities drew commercially from large areas which their rulers did not govern, but which they controlled. Those cities became rich in trade.

The word *city* has two meanings. It means a social organization of individuals performing different functions—carpenters, merchants, police, poets, priests—with a government made up of leaders. It also means the physical shell in which the human group dwells, that is, buildings, streets, plazas, etc. It is important to make this differentiation, because when two ideas are expressed with the same word, we tend to arrive at confused conclusions.

The city made out of people is an organism, and although very primitive, it has unity, and it is alive, which means it re-

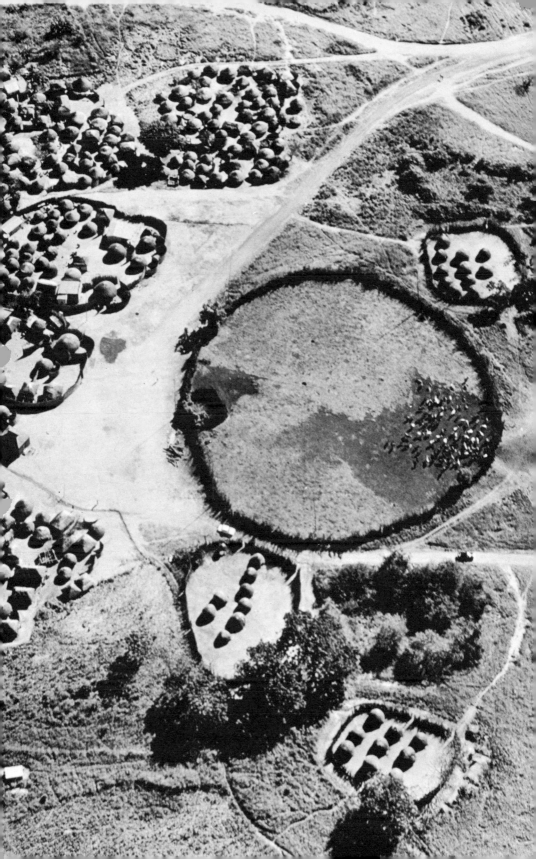

acts, has self-coordination, self-preservation, grows, and multiplies. In the past, human groups often moved from one city
shell to another. In some cases, two different social groups
have lived in a single shell, and in many cases throughout history the same city shell has been inhabited by different groups
at different times. In general, it can be said that the more advanced cultures of the past built handsome shells to dwell in,
and that primitive people dwelt in primitive ones. But it
would be a mistake always to judge people by their city shells,
because in many cases they were not responsible for them.
Conquering armies have always considered city shells an important part of the booty with few exceptions, such as Car-
thage, which the Romans completely destroyed.

Throughout history social groups struggled for power in a
clear evolutionary pattern. A vigorous primitive group, usually under the influence of an enlightened leadership, expands
its territory by conquest, alliances, or commerce. Powerful
and aggressive, it has simple living habits and a strong social
consistency. At some point in its historical development, it
challenges another group considered to be a leading power.
This other group has accumulated wealth, has a looser social
organization, and as a result of feelings of security, has developed high aesthetic standards, and built an attractive city
shell. The vigorous young challenger attacks, and in most cases
is defeated. Only when it is vigorous enough does it win and
conquer.

This pattern of history is clear in the case of Persia and
Alexander, the barbarians and the Roman Empire, the expansion of Islam and the Mongolian invasions toward the
east and the west. It also works from the inside as in the history of China, the French Revolution, or the Russian Revolu-

tion, and can also be applied to the liberation forces of some of the colonial countries.

Young cultures in a period of expansion are not too particular about quality, and their aesthetic standards are poor. When they conquer, they have a primitive concept of reward. It is only after a certain period of development in contact with the more refined culture they have defeated that they notice their clumsiness, and only as they get deeper into the conquered forms of behavior that they understand their meanings. The invaders then begin to admire and eventually to adopt many of the ways and customs of the conquered. They adopt aesthetics physically and intellectually, first as a means of living, and later as an end. It is at this point that the culture produces its best fruits and that the city shell in some cases becomes very handsome. But it is also then, as in the autumn when the leaves are brightly colored and the fruits are ripe, that the end is close. For this is the moment in which cultures are exposed to conquest, peaceful or violent, by strong primitive newcomers whose aggressiveness is stimulated by having little to lose and everything to gain. And the cycle of nature repeats itself like a wheel on a road, going around but always moving ahead. The process is rarely as clear as Alexander invading Persia or the Russian peasants invading the sophisticated Byzantine culture of the Kremlin. In many cases the process is incomplete. In others it is a complex mixture of elements and influences.

Almost all primitive cultures were ruled by king-priests or priest-kings. Man lived always in fear of nature, fear of others, fear of his rulers, and fear of cruel, capricious, revengeful gods. Few people actually lived in the cities—only five or ten percent of the population: the heads of government, some soldiers, merchants, craftsmen, and a good many servants. Cities did not produce any food or materials and consumed large quantities of both supplies and energy. Their function was to serve as interchange and control centers of human societies. (After all, the human brain that serves a similar function takes one-fourth of the total oxygen supplied by the blood, and each one of us wishes his would take even more.)

Cities allied themselves with other cities and cities conquered other cities. In some places one king ruled more than one city, and nations made their first appearance. People accepted kings because they provided security and unity; men could move safely from one city to the other within kingdoms. When later on they found a way of being safe even from their own governments, men could sense that spiritual freedom was near and worked hard to win the final battle in the long process of freeing themselves from their ancestral fears of hunger and other men.

The history of civilization has been the history of societies that lived in cities. Some of them—like the Greeks—had great leaders who gave their people strength and security and who, with intelligence and courage, cleared the weeds and removed the rocks of primitive taboos that millions of years of fear and insecurity had put in the way of man's spiritual freedom. The Greek cities fought the enemy together but never accepted unification by force. A group of simple habits and strong social coherence, the Greeks came from the northeast and settled on the banks of the Mediterranean Sea around the year 1000 B.C. From what other people had done and thought, they made their own selection and drew their own conclusions.

With the Greeks, for the first time, man looked at nature with curiosity rather than fear, and it was from their discovery that man was part of nature that they were able to understand man. This in no way made man's worth any less, on the contrary it made man's more and the gods, less. No other people has ever engendered more power and more dignity for the human race.

Of the many cities the Greeks built, from Asia Minor to Sicily, the most important was Athens, a city originally placed on the rocky mass of the Acropolis. It expanded around the hill and eventually reached the sea at Piraeus. Athens became a commercial power. It organized a defensive league with other cities which eventually paid Athens tribute in money for the privilege of being defended by its fleet. Athens had a very advantageous location for commerce and defense. Having cleared the surrounding seas of pirates, it shone for a period of two or three hundred years with light that has illuminated the western world for over twenty-five centuries.

At the time of Pericles Athens had a population of about 200,000 people, who lived in a concentrated shell of approximately two square miles. This scale made it possible for people, by walking a few blocks, to go to the theater and hear speeches in the assembly or discuss philosophy in the Agora. Since the time of Pericles, Athens' shell has been invaded by the Macedonians and the Romans; it became part of the Byzantine Empire, was invaded by Corinthians, French, Catalonians, Florentines, Venetians, Turks, and the Germans during the last war. From a population of 200,000 people in the year 450 B.C. it dwindled to 4,000 in the year 1834. Today metropolitan Athens has a population close to 2,000,000 people.

Rome achieved unification by force. At the time of Augustus, Rome was a large city of perhaps 700,000 people, and the first metropolis made of several original villages. The Roman Empire encompassed most of the known world (known, that is, to western people at the time) and was the largest political unity the world has ever known. If the Athenians were able to develop man and understand nature to an extraordinary degree, the Romans understood man as a social and political being better than anybody before or after. Their world organization was far more sophisticated than anything existing today. It is sad that the prejudice of Christianity against the Romans has deprived the world of a better understanding of their genius. After all, a history of Rome interpreted by Christians cannot be any better than a history of capitalism written by communists.

For one thousand years after the disintegration of the Roman Empire, the Western world fell back into the primitive culture of men in fear. Man looked for protection, spiritual and physical, and his outlook retrogressed almost to the dawn of civilization. Small, isolated, congested cities cowered behind high walls and wide ditches. Primitive lords buried themselves in big castles, like artificial caves. The Middle Ages was the cultural triumph of the narrow, dark spirit of the catacombs over the humanism of Athens, Alexandria, and Rome.

The world owes to Rome not only the benefits of that great phase of man's history that was the Roman Empire, but also the preservation and diffusion of Greek culture. It also owes to Italy the recovery of men from their darkness of fear and prejudice by the light of humanism. Although it is possible that in time it would have happened elsewhere, the Renaissance happened in Italy. The group of Italian cities that generated the Italian Renaissance communicated with one another and with the world, for they were commercial cities: Venice, Florence, Milan, Rome, Genoa, and at least ten others. All of these were cities of less than 100,000 people, in areas no greater than two square miles, in which people could have direct personal contact and communication with one another. People knew who did what, and in some of these cities some individuals were able to make great contributions in philosophy, science, and art. Among many in Florence alone were Dante, Fra Angelico, Botticelli, Galileo, Cellini, Brunelleschi, Leonardo da Vinci, Michelangelo, Raphael, and Machiavelli. At the time of Lorenzo dé Medici Florence's population was 75,000.

This was also the century of Columbus and Magellan. By the time America was discovered, cannons had already been invented, and city walls had become obsolete. Some kings expanded their territory to large areas containing many cities and corresponding to some of the present European states. Powerful kings, supported by large armies, could guarantee peace and administer justice. People could travel freely within France, Spain, or England. One city became the capital of each state and seat of the government. Italy, Germany, and a few other European countries remained divided into regions, each dependent on an important city. But once kings were able to concentrate great power by creating countries, there was no alternative for the independent cities but unification. By the end of the nineteenth century, the world came to be made of nations, with a few isolated city-states as picturesque anachronisms.

Most cities of the Middle Ages had very high density because they contained a growing population within a defensive wall. In some cases, as population increased, another fortified belt was built farther out, giving the city temporary relief. High density made necessary the utilization of every inch of ground, leaving a minimum of open space, with the result that the streets were narrow, light and fresh air scarce, and sanitary conditions precarious. To add to this, most of the northern cities had not been laid out; the pattern of streets simply grew following old trails, making the cities a labyrinth. These conditions became unbearable when some of the towns grew into large capitals. The invention of the cannon and changes in war strategy during the fourteenth century made defensive walls obsolete, and expansion of cities beyond them feasible. However, the core of the towns remained congested since it contained the buildings and spaces in which the civic, religious, and entertainment activities took place.

Although France had Latin influence on its development, the gridiron street pattern used by the Romans in the layout of their camps and some colonial cities did not affect Paris, which was already established at the time of the Roman invasion of Gaul. The original city of Paris was a fortress on an island in the Seine. Later, towns developed on both sides of the river. It was only in the twelfth century that Paris was organized as a unit. By the year 1600, it was a large city

The Birth of Paris.

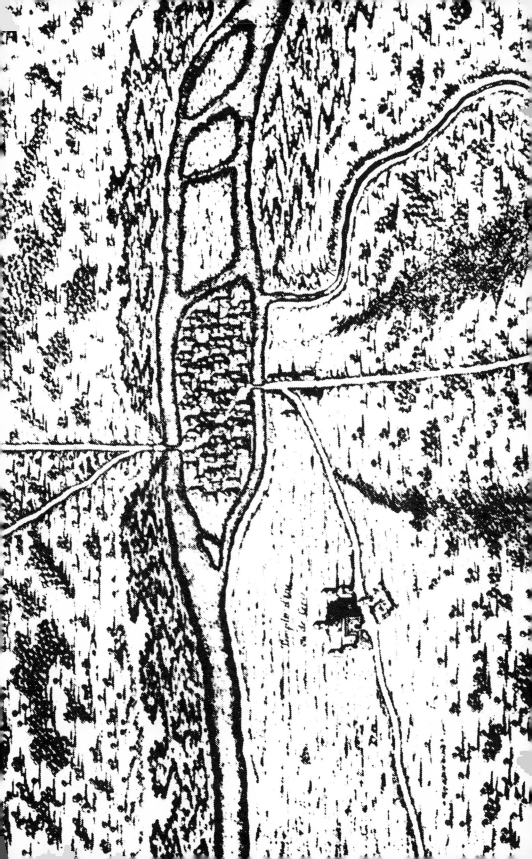

of 350,000 people and divided into sectors, each having its own local sub-center. This was the only solution for a city that had become too large and whose narrow streets and alleys made intercommunication extremely difficult. On the other hand, all major public buildings were located on the central island or in its immediate vicinity.

Louis XIV was very close to the Machiavellian idea of the perfect Renaissance prince. It was he who hated the dark, cluttered, smelly streets of Paris, and moved the government to Versailles, where he could reign in light amid beauty and nature. It was a very dominated nature, in which complicated geometry had been applied to gardens and terraces, for the enjoyment not only of the eyes, but of the intellect. It was under this king in the seventeenth century that the Renaissance reached its summit in France. And ironically enough, it was the seed of enlightenment nurtured by Louis XIV which bore fruit in the minds of Voltaire and Rousseau and eventually in the political and social French Revolution. But it took almost another two hundred years of Renaissance thinking before Paris was made into a Renaissance shell by Napoleon III in the nineteenth century.

In 1848 Louis Napoleon was elected President. Four years later he made himself Emperor of France. The transformation of Paris was his great deed, but as usual, the expense of this enterprise was unimportant compared to that of his international war adventures, of which, of course, nothing remains.

The remodeling of Paris, its transformation into the beautiful city which even today does not have an equal, was done in fifteen years without trucks, bulldozers, or modern earth movers. The procedure by which Georges Eugene Haussmann, Louis Napoleon's Prefect of Paris, executed this incredible job, was in fact less high-handed than the systems

"Boulevard Richard-Lenoir, 1861–63," from *Space, Time and Architecture*, by S. Giedion (Cambridge, 1967). Reprinted by permission of Harvard University Press.

utilized in most of the legalistic democratic societies today for opening freeways. The operation was almost self-financing, and the required subsidy was provided without additional taxes. Funds were handled by an independent board responsible to the legislative body, a board that on many occasions did not approve expenditures and at the end was responsible for Haussmann's resignation. The expropriation board was made up of affected property owners and if there was any complaint it was that the price paid for the property made many of them the *nouveaux riches* of their time.

The magnificent concept of the new Paris had all the qualities of a Renaissance product—obsession with perspective, the three-dimensional concept missing in the Middle Ages; and symmetry, the methodical idea of making two halves equal and placing an element of more importance in the middle, an idea very old in history. Paris expressed also the Renaissance admiration for nature's light and air by bringing gardens and trees into the city, not a fake wilderness but a dominated and intellectualized nature.

Nordic countries then and now have an awe of nature and mystical respect for the plant, the tree of the forest in its natural state. This attitude has expressed itself in the parks of Scandinavia, England, and to a lesser extent the United States. In the north, the green comes only for a short period of the year. Spring means relief from bleak winter. In the European Mediterranean basin, on the other hand, where plants remain green all year, the gifts of nature have always been taken for granted. It was perhaps for this reason that it was there that nature first left the realm of the gods to become the object of man's curiosity. There classical culture was born.

Paris, at the middle of the last century, was the political and cultural center of Europe and a city of almost 1,000,000 people. Napoleon's conception had three principal aims: first, to create straight-line communication between the important points of the city and the central nucleus. This was done through boulevards, some of them planned in the unheard-of width of four hundred feet. The boulevards were conceived as strips of park, to bring nature into the heart of the old city. Planned for both pedestrians and the circulation of vehicles, they restored the city's unity, which growth and congestion had destroyed. The new boulevards made it possible for people to meet with ease, physically and psychologically, beyond the boundaries of their separate quarters. This circulation was also important for defense, since the army and police had by then already started to use heavy equipment on wheels.

The second purpose of the remodeling was to open parks for the common man. Many cities at the time had parks that were originally private gardens or hunting grounds which the nobility, for different reasons, had released for semi-private or public use. In many cases, and this was especially true of London, small parks were part of private urban developments, and their use was restricted. The plan of Paris created large and small green open spaces for everybody. The third aspect of the remodeling was the clearing away of old dilapidated structures clustered around important public buildings. This created pleasant open settings for the buildings and ample space in which people could appreciate them. At the same time it provided protection of the buildings from both riots and fire.

There may have been hundreds of reasons for the remodeling of Paris, but the underlying reason was that one of the most enlightened and sophisticated groups of people of modern times, Paris of the nineteenth century, could not stand the ugliness, darkness, narrowness, and irrationality of an over-grown medieval town. Napoleon III was a shrewd and intelligent politician. Haussmann was an excellent administrator, and a man of great ambition and energy. But if the people had not been behind this incredible enterprise, little would have been accomplished. It was a great solution, in a grand manner. It was wrong only in its concept of timelessness, a concept very much of the Renaissance which did not concern itself with change or evolution. God, nature, man, were all static values organized in such neat intellectual symmetry that there was no room for the dimension of time.

The French rationalism of the seventeenth and eighteenth centuries had found reasons and relations for everything and had all the answers. With religion to fill the gaps, future and past were known and clear. Man was located in the center of the universe in time and space, surrounded by nature and in possession of the only possible instrument of knowledge, human intelligence. Even the great minds of Descartes and Pascal succumbed to this love of balanced perfection on which time and change were intruders. All this was expressed in the plan of Paris and was also present in the political philosophy which produced the American and French revolutions.

During any process, time changes the terms in which that process originated. The bases of any problem become other in time. Often when the change in the factors makes a "perfect solution" irrelevant, the factors are arbitrarily modified or denied, for they cannot be accepted without the destruction of the beautiful concept with which a man, a generation, or a country has fallen in love. This lack of the concepts of time, change, and evolution, can be appreciated very clearly in the plan of Washington, D. C., another European Renaissance city. Washington was planned by L'Enfant fifty years before the renovation of Paris. Because Paris was a city of 1,000,000 people, and the intellectual and artistic center of the world, as well as the seat of one of the major powers of Europe, it was to be the radiant influence, but in fairness Washington should be called the first planned "Renaissance City."

Pierre L'Enfant brought to America from Paris the city planning ideas in vogue at the time. Following a general organization similar to that of Versailles, L'Enfant located the Capitol, where Congress meets, and the residence of the President, seat of the Executive branch of the government, on two intersecting axes, separated by just over one mile. He located the White House on the bank of the Potomac and the Capitol on a hill in the center of the city. (Later on, part of the river bed was filled, leaving the White House a mile away from the river.) The plan of the city was a gridiron of the old Latin type, with large diagonal boulevards converging on the government complex. The two poles were joined by gardens on which the buildings for the judiciary, post office, museums, etc., were to be placed surrounded by the same type of landscaping that made Versailles famous.

Nothing could go wrong with this logical, symmetrical scheme, except that in time the city did not develop in such an intelligent way. Instead, one side, around the village of Georgetown, became fashionable suburbs, while the other, the grounds close to the Capitol, planned for the residences of Congressmen, became dilapidated slums where slaves who escaped from the South during the Civil War made their quarters. The diagonals today, in most cases, join points that have no special need of direct communication. Washington is still a beautiful city. Its generous open space, the gardens of a century ago, have provided convenient locations for more

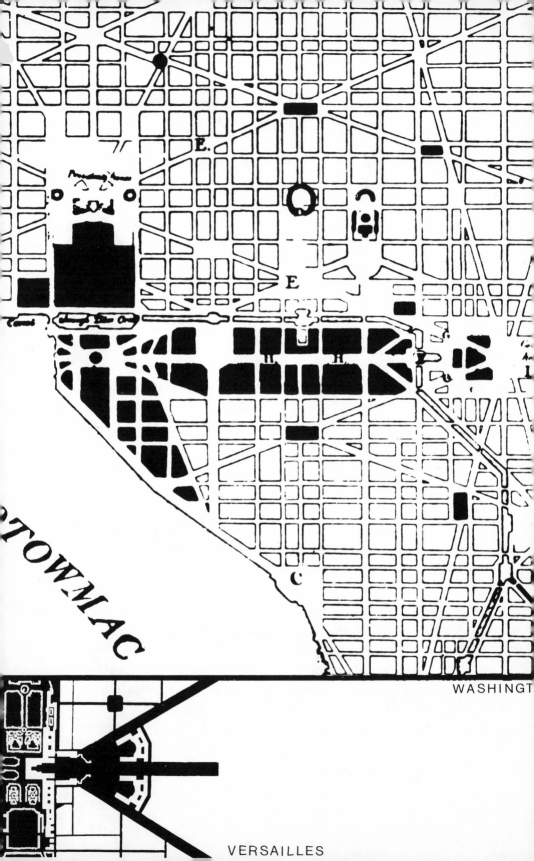

WASHINGT

VERSAILLES

and more buildings for a nation that never thought its capital would become such an important metropolis.

The city was started by George Washington on an area of one hundred square miles, "to leave enough space for growth in the future." (Jefferson thought three square miles sufficient.) Today Washington and suburbs cover an area of more than four hundred square miles. The city of the nineteenth century, the city of the boulevards, was planned for the comfort and enjoyment of the people and also for the circulation of horse carriages, which were then appearing in great numbers as society became affluent. It was so generously conceived in space that when transportation machines appeared, it was able to accommodate them. Only when society became so affluent that everybody could afford an automobile did the boulevards become clogged and the green open spaces become parking lots.

Affluence came to Europe and North America with industry, and industry came with machines. Some of the first machines were for agriculture, the main source of occupation and wealth. The immediate consequence of the mechanization of farms was that the expensive new equipment, efficient only on large tracts of homogeneous cultivation, demanded substantial capital. Banks and city financiers became involved in an industry in which first horses and then men became obsolete.

Displaced farmers began moving to cities in the industrializing countries at about the same time that cities began to change from their ancestral character of citadels and seats of government into production centers. At the beginning cities processed only a few agricultural and mineral products, but by the end of the eighteenth century, iron and steel began to be produced in commercial quantities. Steam was developed

L'Enfant's plan of Washington, D.C., from *Plans and People* (May 1950). Courtesy of the AIA.

as a source of power, making it possible for countries to indus-trialize quickly and on a large scale. The result was that by the nineteenth century some cities of Europe and America had become the main producing areas. For the people, large cities meant a greater range of opportunities and opportuni-ties meant hope and fun. Many were getting rich fast. Big cities meant good pay and lots of places to spend the money. Then industrial cities became crowded. Many people lived in one room in the poor quarters of town. Land prices went up, with rents doubling and redoubling in a single year. Al-though people suffered, few ever returned to their previous occupation on the farms. City living was exciting and drained the farms and small towns of their best and most enterprising youth. Statistics told the story in numbers only.

To depart from the agricultural era has not been easy for man. That the change happened in some of the European countries within one generation made adaptation even more difficult. For the peoples in the Mediterranean basin, the change was not abrupt, since some of them had had large com-mercial cities for many centuries. England, on the other hand, evolved in only one century from a pastoral island of pictur-esque rolling hills and agricultural society into the commer-cial and industrial center of the world. As a result the English people developed a phobia toward cities, and have lived ever since yearning for the pastoral setting which will, of course, never return.

It was in England at the beginning of the nineteenth cen-tury that the railroad was invented and first used. It was also in England in the middle of the century that several societies were founded for the defense of the countryside against the evils of the railroad. Although the building of the British Em-pire belonged to the eighteenth century, the commercial bene-

By Gustave Doré, from *London, A Pilgrimage*, by Gustave Doré and Blanchard Jerrold (London, 1872). Courtesy of The London Museum.

fits were reaped by England during the nineteenth. England developed practical and inexpensive means of producing cast iron and steel for making machines. By the middle of the nineteenth century, England had not only a very large textile industry, but also the sources of fibers on three continents, all transported in its own ships and financed by powerful English banks. To keep this industry moving, England found large sources of coal in its own land. These mines created ugly new towns, of which English writers have been giving us accounts for the last one hundred years. The transformation of the beautiful countryside of the island into a sooty industrial complex was too much for most Englishmen, who since then have considered the city the domicile of everything that is bad and the agricultural countryside the source of everything good.

Not only the countryside was spoiled. The people were degraded by the work in coal mines and factories during the last century: long hours, small remuneration, child labor, appalling physical working conditions, and more than anything else, the feeling of being overcome by the industrial monster without hope of redemption. By 1900, England became the first country in the world with more than half its population in cities. Almost all of the important English literature of the last century was colored by this traumatic experience. It is not strange that the reaction was to go back and build cities in the country. For many years and even today, every move for the improvement of city living in England has been directed toward de-urbanization. The nineteenth century Garden City and the twentieth century Satellite City coincide in this principle.

Streetcars and railroads appeared at the end of the nineteenth century and provided a fast method for selling land along their lines to people yearning for rural living, farm land at the price of urban property. The companies knew that by doing this, they not only made a profit from land but created a forced market of future customers. This was particularly true in England, where the simultaneous expansion of empire and industry created the greatest economic boom the world had known. But it was also true in general of the more advanced countries of Europe and America.

The function of the city in providing security had already been taken over by the nation, and the responsibility of defending people's lives and property from foreign invaders had been centralized. The function of the city as interchange and intercommunication center remained, but with the birth of nations, some of the secondary cities lost importance as armies and revenues became dependent on the central government. The secondary city was still the human social hive, but as the power and wealth left, so did the ambitious young men. Some people could not live too far away from their land, which was their main source of income, and for that reason the smaller city kept its strength, but not for long. As better communications and faster transportation arrived, there was no need for the landowner to be there. His old family house became his country estate. Only the small rural farmer remained.

Industry disrupted not only ways of working and living but the sense of power and values of the world. In one hundred years industry developed from small shops run by humble craftsmen to big industries owned by men of great enterprise, but of very little education, and no understanding of present or past cultures. The balance of social power went berserk. If at one time a rich aristocratic landowner controlled the destiny of one hundred peasants or, in the case of the medieval baron, one thousand or even five thousand, now the industrialist could determine the present and future of millions of workers and consumers. There was a feeling of quantity in the air. Mass production and mass consumption meant more quantity and more and more. The more the better. There was no sense of quality, only quantity, and in many cases at any cost.

In the past, wealth was almost always in land. Wealth in land meant tradition, for only through a long period of time could people accumulate land. Previously, even the best soil with the best care could at most double or perhaps triple its yield. But industry could grow ten times or a hundred times in a short period.

The new industrial development made possible the production of metals at a low price, and for the first time iron and steel could be used in large quantities. The same was true of glass. With steel and glass, tall buildings were built. Concrete, a mixture of lime, sand, and rock, had been used by many people in the past. At the end of the nineteenth century, the substitution for lime of hydraulic cement (which hardens in water) together with the use of steel bars imbedded in the mixture, created a new structural material which, once analyzed and its performance controlled, proved to be very useful, especially in Europe, where steel was costly and labor available.

Today the city has become the center of productivity and in the highly industrialized nations the most important source of wealth, with plants that extract, refine, combine, assemble, manufacture, finish, pack, classify, and distribute everything from fuels to books and from food to intricate mechanisms.

In 1840 an American farmer produced food and fiber enough to feed and clothe four persons; in 1940, himself and eleven others; today himself and 42. From a world of farms with cities, man is moving fast to an urbanized world.

Improved communications today have made it possible for nations to take over the function which once belonged to the city. Some countries are already as homogeneous a group of people as any city of the past ever was. People move within nations with the same ease and freedom as they used to move within an urban area.

The agricultural city man has always known will soon either evolve or disappear. But as it changes first into a large urban area and then into a pan-urban region, society will also change, providing wider and wider horizons for that marvelous product of the evolution of life: man. In some of the more industrialized countries, the change is already there with painful symptoms. But the importance and scope of this step in human development are as exciting and marvelous as the birth of the city was.

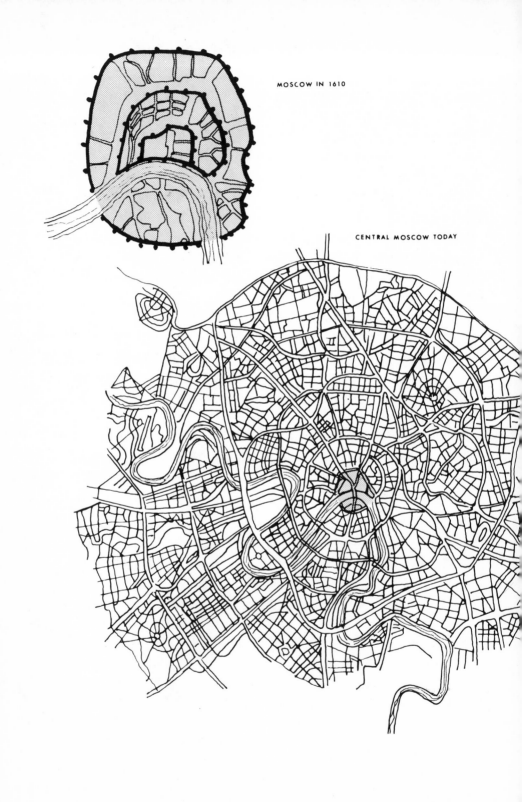

MOSCOW IN 1610

CENTRAL MOSCOW TODAY

INDUSTRIALIZATION

It is not accurate to divide the world into developed and underdeveloped countries. Development is a degree, not a clearly defined condition. Some of the so-called underdeveloped countries are very primitive groups of tribes, while others are sophisticated agricultural societies with a higher degree of cultural development than some industrialized societies. After all, the Greeks of the Golden Age did not have any industry. Industrialization is the proper definition of modern physical achievement. It implies a type of economy which demands sophisticated means of communication, production, and distribution and rapidly brings about a social organization different from the agricultural one with which the world lived for many centuries.

Industrialization in most cases has not come through peaceful evolution. It cost the United States a bloody civil war in which the industrial north imposed its way on the agricultural south. The communist revolution in Russia was a violent transformation of a medieval agricultural society into a modern industrial and scientific state. Industrialization is not necessarily homogeneous. Some countries may have both industrialized regions, with the labor organization and women's independence which have become characteristic of industry, and important cities which derive their subsistence from agriculture and have the corresponding economic and social organization.

Each country, and in some cases, each city has particular characteristics. Nevertheless, to simplify the classification of urban areas they can be divided into three groups.

First, the European city as a prototype. Some of these cities may not be located in Europe and not all of the European cities belong to this group. This is the Renaissance agricultural city, wealthy, in a rapid process of industrialization. It is the city that embodies the finished product of the agricultural era.

Second, the agricultural or commercial pre-industrial cities, some of which belong to the Western world and European traditions, and others to Asian or African cultures, all of them nevertheless influenced by the European Renaissance city. These cities, to a much lesser degree than the first group, are shifting to industry as the main source of income and occupation. They are following the European and American patterns of development, and their people are impatient.

Finally, the American city as a prototype. Most of the cities of the United States were shaped and many were born in the industrial and scientific age which took over America before any other country. Because of this influence, nowhere in the world can the impact of the industrial and scientific age on cities be better appreciated or its lessons better learned.

The cities of Europe remained basically medieval in character until the beginning of the nineteenth century, when industry overlapped with colonial empires and created the great wealth that made it possible to remodel the shells, by opening boulevards, plazas, and parks, creating today's handsome European capitals. The nucleus of the present European metropolis corresponds in most cases to the original medieval town. The city grew in concentric rings around it, and left in each the marks of important events in buildings, monuments, streets, and plazas, rich not only in historical but in spiritual content. In the past most government, religious, commercial, and civic activities took place in the nucleus, usually in monumental buildings. Residences clustered around this nucleus, with the large and important near the center and the small and poor on the periphery. As the cities grew in population, they tended to expand. Since for reasons of convenience and prestige nobody wanted to move farther from the nucleus, the city was always subjected to a strong centripetal force. Not until the last century did inside pressure expand the city beyond walking distances, creating the need for transportation. Cities then grew along the routes of the newly built tramways and railroads, and began to take the shape of large spiders which they have today.

Government offices, important private companies, museums, cathedrals, restaurants, theaters, night clubs, and main shopping areas are still located close to the heart of the European capitals, all in a relatively small area, and all within walking distance. Centrally located high-rise apartments and hotels make it possible for those living there to walk to the core along pleasant, ample, landscaped boulevards. The great charm of these cities consists of this concentration which makes strolling in a dense, handsomely built, and busy area a very exciting experience.

Most of the scientific discoveries of the eighteenth and nineteenth centuries took place in Europe. Consequently, industrialization, improvement in health with the resulting increase of population, and the shift from rural to urban ways of living, all happened more or less simultaneously. Industry and population had a parallel growth. Factories in the cities used the rural labor surplus which, with very few exceptions, such as Ireland, never accumulated on the farms. Because Europe never had an important shortage of labor, industrialization was not forced to rapid development through labor-saving techniques as it was in the United States. In Europe as a whole, the percentage of rural population remained larger than the urban until World War II. Today in Europe only sixty percent of the population is urban, compared to eighty percent in the United States. And so Europe has a large reservoir of people in rural areas or small towns who will soon be moving toward the important cities.

Many cities were destroyed or badly damaged by air bombing during World War II. Reconstruction took place rapidly, unfortunately very much on the same prewar patterns. From 1946 to the present, Europe has rebuilt and expanded its industrial plants with more efficient equipment and better systems of production. Common markets are creating mass consumption on a scale Europe has never known. Salaries and purchasing power are on their way up. People want individual mechanical transportation. At the beginning they were satisfied with small motorcycles, but as the economic bonanza continued, automobiles in large numbers appeared. In the fifteen years between 1948 and 1963, the number of automobiles in Europe increased from 5 million to 34 million. These machines, which occupy over one hundred square feet at rest and use one thousand times more space as they move, create the congestion well-known today in Paris, Rome, or Copenhagen.

To accommodate a fast-growing population, including a yearly flood of tourists and labor migration from other countries, and to cope with so many automobiles, the European city has to expand in size, and as it expands it will need even more mechanical transportation. The fact that people in the future will have more automobiles will stimulate decentralization and will induce the growth of neighborhood commercial centers. Although some of the centrally located points of attraction of these cities are of course irreplaceable and will always constitute an important reason to go to the central core, decentralization and suburban living, "American style," will eventually invade Europe as it reaches the two-automobile-per-family stage. Full regional neighborhood activities require an automobile for the man to drive to work, and at least another for family use during the day.

Some European countries have already planned decentralization through satellite communities—small, rather concentrated cities of 20,000 to 200,000 people with their own civic and commercial facilities. Some of these satellite cities are basically residential and in fact can be called suburbs, but others have been planned as complete cities with residences and industry to provide housing and work within a short distance. As for the future form of the European urban areas, it is an unknown, for it will be determined by the mounting and still ungauged forces which are in the process of creating a unified Europe.

Ninety percent of the world still lives in the agricultural era. Non-industrialized cities are located on all continents and they range from extremely sophisticated communities to primitive settlements; from large international centers to rural towns; from very rich to very poor; and their traditions vary from Asian and African to pre-Columbian American and European. Their only common ground is that the basis of the livelihood of the people and their corresponding outlook are not industrial. The shift from agriculture to industry is as important in the history of man as the change from hunting to agriculture was. With agriculture, wandering tribes became communities. All of the countries of the world are in a process of urbanization and all of the cities of the world are suffering a traumatic adaptation, but for the non-industrialized cities, the process has become a tragic experience.

Not too long ago, at the beginning of the century, cities were peaceful and pleasant residences for ten to fifteen percent of the population of a country. Today the national population is in many cases three or four times greater and the cities now represent forty to fifty percent of the total. At the beginning of the century ten people lived in the cities and ninety on farms; today there are 120 in the cities, or twelve times the urban population of fifty years ago, and 180 on the farms, or twice as many. As population continues to grow and the proportion of urban over rural continues to increase, the crowding of cities intensifies and constitutes one of the most important social problems of the world today.

The increase in the rate of population growth in Europe and the United States occurred over a period of one hundred years as the control of infectious diseases improved. To the agricultural countries it came all at once when large and universal health campaigns became possible. This increase found Europe already in the process of urbanization, with the lowest reproduction rate in the world. In the non-industrialized nations it made its impact on a population eighty to ninety percent rural. Many of these countries are located in the tropics and subtropics, where reproduction rates are the highest. Most of these countries depend on agriculture or mineral production of raw materials either with primitive tools and systems, or with modern means but in partnership with industrialized nations. Agricultural output in some of them has not increased in proportion to population in the last thirty years because the rise in rural labor cost has tended to paralyze expansion. In many, production cannot increase to any important degree without a complete revolution in farming, such as the utilization of modern equipment and scientific methods of cultivation, both of which demand capital, transportation, distribution, storage facilities, and tracts of land large enough to make modernization economically feasible. Such agriculture, similar to that of the industrialized countries, requires very few people. So, if there is now overpopulation in the rural areas, the future, progress or no progress, holds more overpopulation for those areas in spite of the large migration to the cities. And this overpopulation is already very high. Venezuela, for instance, which has a proportion of farmers smaller than many other Latin American countries, had in 1961 seventy-eight males per square mile occupied in agriculture, compared to seven in the United States.

In the cities the situation is just as bad. The large migration of unskilled peasants piles up on the fringes of the cities. Unable to purchase or rent, they build shacks on any peripheral empty land, private or public, from which they are not expelled by force. That land is usually the most undesirable from the sanitary and transportation points of view. There are shanty towns in practically all the cities of the unindustrialized countries of the world. One extreme example is in Calcutta where 700,000 migrants from East Pakistan created one of the lowest urban living standards in modern history: fifty-seven percent of the population of Calcutta's three million have one room per family. In some sections twenty-one people share a primitive latrine. The new nations of Africa are only beginning to urbanize, but present conditions in some of those cities augur that the worst urban slums in the world are yet to come.

The city slums in the non-industrialized countries are no worse than their farm slums. If it is true that shacks under the trees are more picturesque, they are nonetheless shacks. If the conditions of rural living seem more attractive, in fact they are not, or migration would move in the opposite direction. These cities vary a great deal since the non-industrialized population of the world encompasses all kinds of people living under all kinds of conditions. Appalling as the *favelas* of Rio de Janeiro or the slums of Caracas are, they are so only in relation to the glamorous cities in which they are located. Such is not the case of the cities in other countries where the general physical and human standards are similar to those of the *favelas* or shanty towns of Latin America. But what is true of all is that to a smaller or greater extent they are becoming depositories of the world's enormous population overflow that cannot go anyplace else.

If the new population of the cities could rapidly achieve a high standard of living, it would automatically begin to reduce its birth rate. Urban population with low standards, however, multiplies with almost the same speed as that of peasants. Mexico City has raised its standard of living in the last few years very rapidly. Between 1940 and 1960, fifty percent of the population increase of Mexico City was multiplication. The rate of increase is now diminishing so steadily that by 1970 it became half what it was in 1950.

Most of these cities have the typical anatomy of the agricultural urban shell with a nucleus in which all important functions take place. The people live around it, with the best toward the center and the worst toward the periphery, except that modern transportation has caused some changes in the urban structure. The bulk of the growth piles up on the edges, while the main body of the city is compressed and the nucleus is more and more congested. With the exception of some small commercial and neighborhood facilities, important activities remain located in the core. Large masses of people move in and out every day on deficient and overcrowded public transportation. Density is high, land use intense, and land prices in the core very high. Central residential areas are rebuilt with multi-family dwellings that increase density and congest the nucleus even more. Land and buildings are the safest and most profitable financial investment. As the city becomes more crowded and more dense, real estate prices increase, stimulating even more density and crowding.

The cities of the unindustrialized countries cannot extend beyond their means, and their means are very small. Very few can afford the construction of underground transportation. Few of their citizens can afford private vehicles. Automobiles imported or locally assembled have prices two or three times higher than in the industrialized nations, and so constitute a great luxury. Wealthy people, who can afford automobiles, have been moving out of the cities during this century, and have built exclusive residential areas beyond the unsightly outskirts. These residential sections have their own commercial facilities and constitute suburban islands similar to typical neighborhoods of the cities of the industrialized countries.

Most of the unindustrialized cities of the world have some manufacturing. Many of them have developed industry of the type the wealthy countries of Europe and America started with, such as textiles and steel. But the most important industry is construction which can use raw labor, and absorbs the largest percentage of unskilled peasants. Construction has created many satellite industries that employ some skilled labor, so in even the least industrialized countries there are today more jobs and higher salaries in the large cities than in the small towns and rural areas.

There is also a certain amount of industrialization of basic consumer items. But all gains are wiped out daily by pressure to keep up with the new products of the industrialized nations, and by the need to purchase abroad expensive equipment, such as jet airplanes, which can be manufactured only by countries with plenty of know-how, capital, and markets. Industrialization requires capital investment, but with the high rate of population growth, more urgent needs consume any capital surplus. The chances of industrialization on any important scale are consequently small.

In the industrially advanced countries, production is rapidly entering a scientific phase in which highly sophisticated equipment and new sources of energy demand highly trained workers, performing in cooperation with scientists and computers in automated plants. This situation requires not only enormous capital but long years of education to produce college graduates who form the labor force. How can the unindustrialized countries hope to accomplish this feat?

Urbanization has mistakenly been thought to be the cause of these problems. In fact, it is a reflex defense. It is easier for people to be educated and to become productive and responsible citizens when they are concentrated in cities than when they are scattered about the countryside—among other reasons because their needs are more apparent. With better salaries and more education, a middle class becomes important in size and political power. It is true that this is the class that demands most. Since communications today have made the world one, and international audio-visual material most often originates in the most industrialized countries, people all over the world are kept in a continuous state of stimulation and appetite for more and better things. This healthy desire for progress maintains hope but at the same time generates frustration, as the cities are unable to supply the standards people see in television, movies, or magazines. Cities can barely offer minimum services. Any improvements in water supply, electricity, or public transportation achieved through painful effort are canceled by the continuous increase in population.

As a result of the exorbitant population growth, the cities of the non-industrialized countries are forced to spend large sums of money to provide minimum housing, sanitary facilities, and public services for masses of people who cannot contribute taxes. The result is municipal bankruptcy, more and higher taxes and sacrifices for the small wealthy groups, and discontent from everybody. Uprisings, riots, revolutions push the defenseless peasants even faster to the cities where they feel more secure. The world is in turmoil as a result of the slow but fatal move toward the enjoyment of the benefits of industrialization, not for a minority of powerful countries or a minority of powerful individuals in the countries, but for everybody. This will come no matter how many changes have to be made in the political, social, and financial structure of the world.

The gap between the two types of economy is widening at staggering speed. The world has experienced in only a few years a situation similar to the one that took hundreds of centuries back at the dawn of civilization, when agricultural communities prospered far ahead of the wandering, hunting tribes. Many of the unindustrialized countries are products of recent colonial administrations or correspond to the territory of local revolutionary leaders. Many of them do not have unity, others are too small to be efficient in an industrialized world, and very rarely do they correspond to a logical geographical region. In fact, most of them are imitations of the European nations of the nineteenth century. But Europe had a long and hard process of evolution from medieval cities with their small surrounding regions, to countries, and today to the European Common Market which will make possible survival in a world of united republics or states.

The isolated state will become as obsolete as the isolated city became two centuries ago. Just as nations like France once became unfair competition to cities like Venice or Florence and eventually forced their agglutination into countries, new groups of states like Russia, the United States, the People's Republic of China, are forcing others to form federations large enough to support massive industrial development. Most of the unindustrialized countries were born and are still being born politically and economically obsolete.

U.S.A., THE COAST-TO-COAST TOWN

The United States of America and industrialization were born at the same time. In peaceful and orderly development the nation has made the industrial era fit its own shape. Except for the economic depression during the nineteen thirties, the country has not suffered any major calamity since the Civil War, more than one hundred years ago. International wars have taken place outside its continental territory, and have actually been stimulating for the development of better industrial tools and scientific methods. Having plenty and varied resources of raw materials, and being constantly enriched by an immigration of hard-working people with great ambition and in some cases high intelligence, the United States has been phenomenal in its development. Political freedom, freedom of movement within and among the states, freedom from traditions, freedom from social and economic barriers, have created a very enterprising group, and a country of great vitality and enormous wealth.

The European countries, regions, and cities grew up isolated for many centuries. Many of them developed separate cultures, customs, and languages. The picturesque and pleas-pleasant variety found in Europe and in some other parts of the world is lacking in the United States. Although there are some traces of accent and a few regional traditions, the visitor finds the same behavior in the people from Maine to California and from Oregon to Florida. The differences, and there are some, are basically of climate. Variations of culture and tradition, although important to the native, are too subtle for the visitor.

In Europe, the Frenchman, the Spaniard, and the German not only speak differently, but have different-looking cities. Their living rooms at home are not alike, and what is more important, they have a different set of reflex reactions. They laugh at different jokes, females display different attributes to attract males, and people have disparate concepts of what perfection is in human beings and things. It can be said that the only aspect recognizable as common to the various European cities today is a certain "Americanization" that in recent years has invaded hotels and tourist places.

Americanism is a culture with a very strong flavor that exists in every part of the United States. So strong and so evenly spread is this culture throughout the nation that it has largely covered over Americans' countries of origin and religious beliefs. With few and very particular exceptions, people as individuals or as groups react in the same way to the same stimuli. Females react in a similar manner to men's territory and power. People eat and like the same kinds of food. Their goals are similar and so is their judgment of objects and events. Americans are so much alike that even violent disagreement among them implies only different positions for aiming at the same target.

At the beginning the United States tended to form two types of culture, but the Civil War erased this trend toward differentiation. The industrialized North defeated the agricultural South. This sort of unified culture existed in the past only within a city and usually, only within a group in that city. The United States is the largest homogeneous culture the world has ever known. The railroad, telephone, and telegraph appeared at the time when the nation was very young, when pioneers were moving in search of places to settle. Later came the automobile, the airplane, radio, movies, and television. In a climate of availability of things and abundance of communications, people continued to move in search of opportunities. Mass industrial production helped to create even standards of taste. Common ideals of wealth became common standards of success. Movies and television together with newspapers and popular novels exploit, via mass production, a mass audience with standardized reflexes.

The great cultures of the past were achieved in a few cities whose small scale and population allowed intercommunication. People could go from one place to another. People could hear and see what others said or did. Most of these characteristics have been achieved in America as a whole. The country has almost complete and instant communications.

The nation is attempting to wage a war against prejudice, ignorance, poverty, and injustice in a medium of economic abundance. For the first time in the history of man a nation the size of a continent is trying to achieve freedom from the fear of hunger, other men, and cruel revengeful gods. Such conditions should have, as in the past, expressed themselves in physical beauty. In the United States they do not. Instead, what is man-made reflects the clumsiness of a fast-growing, powerful nation, pioneering into the industrial and scientific age, handsome because of its youth and power and homely because of its insecurity, a country in which commercialism has spread like a bad weed. The cities have a monotonous commercial appearance. Rivers, lakes, and air are polluted by chemicals and waste, and most roads are lined with billboards and cheap, gaudy buildings. It can be said, in general, that what remains beautiful in the country are the natural features that man has not yet touched, because they either lack commercial possibilities or have been preserved as public property.

There is a natural land formation along the east coast which practically triples the shoreline of the Atlantic Ocean by creating an inland waterway. Both ocean and waterway are beautiful and enjoyable, the first for beach and bathing, the second for sailing and boating. Florida alone, counting its islands, has a shoreline of 8,426 miles. But ocean drives and seaside restaurants with open views and terraces, common in the rest of the world, are practically nonexistent. Restaurants, even beside the sea, are enclosed, artificially lighted, standardized eating places that could be anywhere. They have no windows because there is usually nothing to look at except signs large and small, telephone and electric poles, wires, and more cheap-looking buildings like themselves.

Most cities in the United States are ugly. Some of the old country towns in the East and Middle West are handsome and a few are very beautiful. In New England, some of the small towns have dignity and are probably the most beautiful, but there too, the growing industrial towns and large cities are disorganized and ugly. Some residential districts in almost every major city have the beauty and quality of the traditional American small town. But the extension of the unattractive in those cities has become so immense that the attractive has become insignificant. Many people have classified the typical American city of today as a "sub-city," a city without a soul, a conglomeration of suburbs, most of them dilapidated.

On many occasions the automobile has been blamed for the overextension and shambles of the cities in the United States, and its extermination has been suggested as the remedy. This is as logical as blaming umbrellas for the rain. The abolition

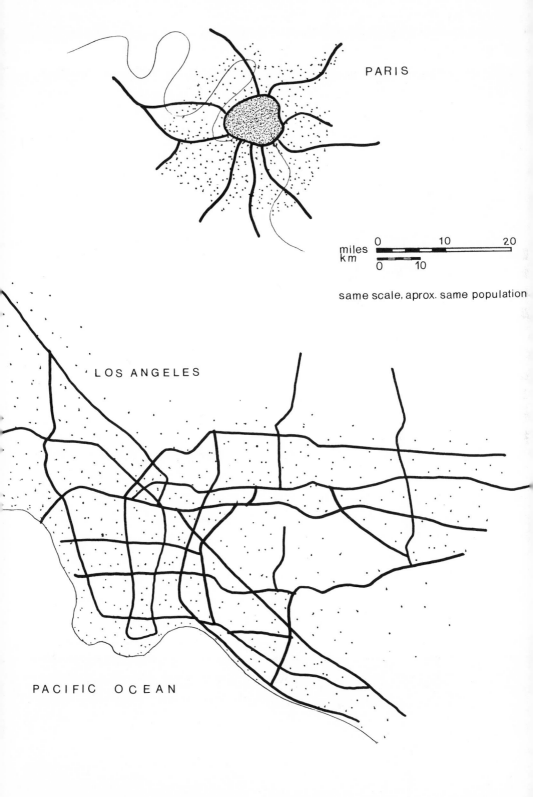

PARIS

miles
km

0
0

10

10

20

same scale, aprox. same population

LOS ANGELES

PACIFIC OCEAN

of umbrellas would be just as practical and effective in the control of weather. If the automobile is responsible, so are the telephone, television, and refrigerator. The characteristics of the American city are the result of the unbridled force of industry and science, and of their impact on communications and services, not for a small minority, but for everybody.

Railroads and streetcars created paths of expansion in the over-dense cities of Europe during the last century. Electric lines ran along those same routes. Most of the cities of the United States were born at that time and their development also took place along the lines of public transportation and electricity. In Europe those lines were like spider legs converging on a nucleus, but in many American cities there was very little nucleus or there were many undeveloped nuclei, for by then centralized urban services and administration were beginning to lose their reason for existence.

There were also social and cultural causes for the uncontrolled development of American cities. The pioneers brought with them the puritanical ideas of the time, most of which were basically rural. Suspicious of the concentration of power in popes and kings, they favored the small village over the city, and the work done with one's own hands over the philosophical and aesthetic refinements of a society based on servants. The pioneer was a rural man, a farmer who prized his independence and freedom above everything else. The small group of gentlemen interested in what the world was thinking lived in a few places on the East Coast. These gentlemen interpreted the sentiments of their time and gave the country the principles of the Constitution, with which it has lived since. This same group created Washington with the French concepts of city planning. But it was Jefferson's dislike of

large cities that made him suggest three square miles as a
good size for the capital. He also liked rural societies.

Immigration to the United States during the nineteenth
century was mostly of farmers who readily took up the pioneer spirit, and of a few discontented Englishmen, running
away from the reckless industrialization of their island. No
wonder then, that when industrialization took over the country, pulling people from farms to cities, the American farmer
brought his ideals and his way of living to the city with him,
and the cities became a sprawled conglomeration of mini-
farms with farmers who worked in industry or business during the week and did their farming in their gardens Satur-
days and Sundays. However, this is only part of the story.
After the Civil War, the industrial revolution took hold of
the country. Industry brought with it new principles, most
of them the antitheses of the puritanical precepts of the rural
pioneer. Efficiency and competition became the gods of industrial free enterprise. Money became synonymous with
success. It could be made fast by those who had the drive and
the talent, and were ruthless enough. Once independent farmers, the majority of the people became workmen in factories
and offices, always yearning for their lost independence which,
in their minds, could be regained only through the acquisi-
tion of money. As the United States became the land of high
salaries and of the many things to be bought with them, a
new type of immigrant arrived from European cities, who
soon became an entrepreneur himself.

If the European city was affected by the railroad, the streetcar, and electricity in the hands of the same traditional
groups who had previously controlled the land, the American
city became an orgy of millions of enterprises mostly in the
hands of ignorant promoters who inherited from the origi-

nal pioneer farmer only his zeal for independence. Laws made for a slow-paced agricultural society became useless in a fast-moving industrial economy. The impact on the cities was a calamity. A few of the older cities had already formed a nucleus similar to that of European urban centers. These were able to withstand the impact without completely losing their urban integrity. They were New York, Philadelphia, San Francisco, and a few others that had a concentration of important services in monumental buildings erected during the agricultural era. In cities that were born, or that became important, after the impact of industry, the nucleus remained undeveloped, for by then it was not essential. The city grew, guided only by the anarchy of individual enterprise in search of profit.

As the country became wealthier, and more urbanized, the consumer, stimulated by advertising, began to demand more. The ideals of the urbanized farmer became closer to those of the country gentleman. If the original pioneer did not want a servant class, industry, with high salaries, made it impossible to have one. Electricity became the servant, and as wealth grew, so did enterprise in the creation of small practical machines to free women from domestic tasks.

The automobile was produced largely to answer the demand for a vehicle that would free men from the care of horses in a land without servants. For in the growing towns and the large cities, a wealthy country was already riding in horse carriages by the millions, and the traffic jams caused then by private landaus, phaetons, and truck wagons in New York, Philadelphia, and Boston were as bad as or worse than those caused today by automobiles. With the automobile the last vestiges of the centripetal force which had held the American city to a nucleus were broken and, in a booming economy, the cities expanded, supported by unlimited production of electricity, oil, cement, lumber, and machines.

The important cities of the past had been carefully carved during many years of history. The basic principles of defense and of centralized services and entertainment had created over the years handsome organic shells. By the time mechanized transportation arrived, the cities of Europe already had such an important nucleus that even when they sprawled in new suburbs, the centripetal force of the nucleus held and the daily flow of people from periphery to center and back continued to be basic in their lives. From this arose the importance of public transportation in those cities, without which they could never inhale and exhale the masses of daily commuters. But the average American city today has so many nuclei, and its main lines of communication are scattered over such large areas, that the automobile is as essential as the telephone or electric service.

New York and San Francisco have a centralized nucleus, in and out of which people move daily, and more than any other American cities resemble their European counterparts. The nucleus contains in high density the major points of attraction in business, civic activities, theater, restaurants, and shops, surrounded by hotels and high density residential apartments. Distances within the nucleus are relatively short, and people not only walk there, but enjoy walking in an urbane atmosphere. People in both these places feel very proud of their cities and in both, some of them take special care to present themselves well-dressed while strolling in the streets. As in the European cities, it is relatively easy for people to make personal contacts. Businessmen, professionals, and artists meet and mix at lunch or other social gatherings in an almost daily routine. It is quite obvious that these two cities are special cases. Something made it possible for them to continue a trend similar to that of their European counterparts in spite of the disruption of the development of the agricultural city in the United States by the impact of industrialization more than one hundred years ago. There is an explanation. Both Manhattan and San Francisco are surrounded by water and had their development contained by a barrier similar to the walls of the European medieval town. When bridges were built, these two cities sprawled over the countryside. The sprawl itself, the city beyond the original town, has followed, in both New York and San Francisco, the typical pattern of the American city.

These two examples of urbanity and European cultural sophistication are in fact products of an unusual geographical condition that made it possible for the European agricultural city to develop with its typical characteristics far into another era. These two cities and some others to a lesser degree are living anachronisms, dinosaurs that are finding survival difficult in changing vegetation.

The typical American city, amorphous and sprawled, is ugly and has many unsolved problems, but its life does not depend on the closing of a few bridges or tunnels by bombs, labor strikes, or mechanical failures. Although the urban sprawl of the American city would have been impossible without the present development of industry and science applied to urban living, the typical American city is less vulnerable and can survive longer without electricity or transportation than concentrated New York or San Francisco, or for that matter, the European or Japanese metropolis. The old American pioneering instinct for independence has proved to be wise.

The typical American city is not, in fact, a city; it is a pan-urban region, a conglomeration of cities, suburbs, and semi-urbanized areas loosely set together, among which there is little social unity.

The typical city of the past could not have survived without centrally located government, civic, commercial, and entertainment facilities. The new pan-urban region in the United States does not require this centralization at all. Contact with the government is made by mail or telephone. Civic and business meetings are in no way circumscribed to local areas. Many people in Los Angeles or Miami visit New York, Washington, or Chicago, thousands of miles away, more often than the downtown sections of their own city. Very few things are not available in the suburban centers: banks, insurance companies, restaurants, theaters, are all near the places where people live. And the best and largest are rarely located in the central city; they are in the suburbs, and people may drive twenty miles for the theater or restaurant of their preference. Suburban living as practiced today in the United States is possible only with a high degree of political and industrial sophistication.

The pan-urban formation is a recent phenomenon occurring with particular exuberance in the warmer regions of the country, such as California, Arizona, Texas, and Florida, where the enjoyment of nature is possible twelve months of the year. Until very recently, because there was no practical way to combat excess heat in climate, people preferred the northern part of the country. Today air conditioning has opened the South. The climate once good for cotton or seasonal vacationing has become ideal all year around. The new temperate pan-urban formations have brought with them a new suburb-centered way of living which implies a type of house, of clothing, of car, and a type of social behavior. The swimming pool, the grand luxury of the last century, has become the common denominator in suburbia.

With incomes growing at the rate of five percent per year, more people can afford swimming pools, two or three cars per family, boats, and golf club memberships. More people than ever have savings, pensions, and income for early retirement. People have more leisure and with highly automated industry will soon have even more. This new kind of suburb provides a feeling of freedom, of independence, of relaxation, that people like. One can avoid the sight of the large decaying sectors of the American city. Density in these new areas is very low, and automobile traffic relatively simple except for the main interregional arteries which are now being made into multi-lane freeways. Public transportation is unimportant. These cities are not the last century's spiders whose defined lines of crucial communication public transportation could serve efficiently or economically. Walking is a rare activity except on the golf course or in the shopping center. But even there people do not like to walk, witness the golf cart. Statistics show that the average person would rather drive ten miles to shop than walk ten blocks.

Today this is the way of life most people in the United States want. It is the one portrayed in movies, glamorous television programs, and advertising. That the pan-urban formations are growing faster than any other areas in the United States seems to confirm this. Seventy-four percent, seventy-nine percent, and forty-eight percent are the figures for the increases of population in Arizona, Florida, and California during the postwar decade of the fifties, compared to sixteen percent, ten percent, and thirteen percent for Illinois, Massachusetts, and New York. The purpose for which the ancestral centralized city was created no longer exists. The security once based on the walls of the European medieval town is located for the United States in the air and sea all over the earth and in satellites beyond earth.

New systems of communication have made it possible for people to live together 3,000 miles apart. Today when a man hears a voice or music on his radio, he doesn't know and he doesn't care whether it is coming from a few blocks or thousands of miles away. A man lectures in Boston in the afternoon and in the evening in Miami. Retail sales throughout the country are made from warehouses in a few states.

On the average, the American family changes residence within the nation with the same ease that people used to move from one house to another within a city: once every four years. It is rather unusual to find people living in the locality where they were born. The population within the country flows steadily in search of better opportunities. This flow will continue to increase as transportation and communications improve.

It is not fair to compare the great agricultural or commercial metropolises of Europe, such as Paris, Rome, Stockholm, or Vienna, with the typical American city. Those are finished products of many centuries of refinement in city living and city building. They were shaped by physical and spiritual forces applied during many centuries under the intelligent direction of elites. The American city is new, the forces that are shaping it are still changing, and its shape is far from a final product. Bad as it is, it is very important, for it contains the germs of the city of the future.

This discussion probably brings to many people's minds Los Angeles as a prototype of the American city of the future, and it is good that it does. For unless American urban forces are properly understood and guided, instead of denied or ignored, and unless the development of the city is taken out of the hands of the land traders, money lenders, and engineers, that is exactly the way the United States will look a few years from now: a gigantic urban minestrone.

Metropolitan areas in the United States are not political units. Almost all of them are agglutinations of municipalities around a central city, from which the total often derives its name. Miami, for instance, is actually twenty-seven municipalities and a large unincorporated area, all loosely held together by a metropolitan authority. Few other areas have even that much governmental unity. Even within the same hive, competition among the cities is often ruthless. Many of the new urban developments are made into cities for the selfish tax advantage of residents or promoters. The result is a competition in which the central cities are losing, for as the people move out to newer neighborhoods, aggressive business moves after them. The central city is withering like a plant without water. Neighborhoods that flourished twenty years ago are dying today, victims of the economic growth and fast metabolism of a society trained to throw away the old model and replace it with the new.

In the old agricultural city the nucleus exercised a strong centripetal force that held the urban organism together and made over-extension difficult. Renovation took place continuously and automatically as a result of the pressure created by growth within a limited area and the consequent rise in land values. The slums and shanty towns in the poorest cities of the world, located in the periphery, are usually cleaned out as the city slowly expands. These self-renewal processes

Core of a typical American city (Salt Lake City), by J. M. Heslop, from *The New City*, by The National Committee on Urban Growth Policy. Used by permission of J. M. Heslop.

still function in many European cities, the cities of the un-industrialized countries, and in the United States in places like Manhattan where, because of geographical limits to extension, old or deteriorated sections are rebuilt with better structures. The typical American city lacks such an automatic clearing mechanism and, together with the newest and best, has urban derelict areas which, as time goes by, increase and become larger. In many of the important metropolitan areas these derelict sections account for fifty percent of the total and as much as eighty percent of the central city.

For many years poor white farm laborers from the country and from abroad arrived in the urban areas and found inexpensive shelter in the discarded sections near the core. Lacking automobiles, the foreign immigrants found this central location surprisingly economical compared to what it would cost abroad, and made their quarters in what became Irish, Italian, Chinese, or Spanish sections. But as the children of those people became assimilated to a new form of living, those sections were emptied.

Europe is now using its excess of rural population in its own industrial expansion, stimulated by the common markets. Laws have restricted immigration to the United States of large rural groups from Asia or Africa, and unless South America becomes a new source, there will no longer be important groups of poor rural foreigners in the urban derelicts.

The American white farmer, who one hundred years ago formed eighty percent of the population, today makes up less than five percent. His last important migration to the cities took place during the depression and the dust storms of the thirties and forties. The white slum in America is on its way out. The derelict areas are being partially filled by the last immigrant from the American farms, the blacks. Because of its characteristics, this group will take longer to be assimilated, but within this century the black slum may also disappear.

The blacks remained on the farms until World War II, after which few black soldiers or war workers returned to rural areas. Since then, the large reservoir of poor black farm labor has been moving to the cities. Forty-two percent of the sharecroppers of Alabama, Arkansas, Florida, Louisiana, Mississippi, North and South Carolina, and Tennessee, moved to urban areas between 1959 and 1964. By 1969, only one million blacks lived on farms, or five percent, the same figure which holds for the general population. It can be said that in spite of the appalling state of the slums in many American cities, the living conditions of the individuals are generally better than they were where they came from.

Urban derelict areas do not necessarily become slums. One hundred eighty thousand Cuban refugees settled in Miami from 1960 to 1968. This immigration was made up of mostly urban people with professional or business occupations, for whom the change was a hard step down from apartments or single dwelling units in Cuba to houses rented by the room in the United States. They came precisely at the end of a post-war building boom. The over-expansion of south Florida had created large derelict areas around the central cities, especially Miami, with the result that many sections built only twenty-five years before were already decaying. The Cuban refugees moved in and revived and improved the decaying central area. They may eventually return to Cuba, or assimilate American standards and move to the suburbs, generating derelict areas again as they move out.

In spite of the language barrier, the Cubans have adapted quickly to the American way of living because of their education and urban background. If the immigration had been of rural labor, it would have taken more than one generation. If it had been black, prejudice would have erected a communications barrier, causing this adaptation to take longer still. Ignorant rural labor with low standards of living move into derelict urban areas for the simple reason that they cannot afford any other. Their earning capacity is very low. As a result of the application of their primitive rural standard to such areas, the slum appears.

But contrary to general thinking which holds that the decay of American cities is created by pockets of poverty, the eradication of which will improve the urban shell, the growing decay in the cities is created not by poverty but by wealth. The more prosperous the population and the larger the percentage that can move in search of better dwellings and urban surroundings, the more urban derelicts there will be and the more dilapidated the cities will look.

Poverty has to be fought on the battlefield of economics. Poor people do not create the deterioration of the cities. Poor people move to the derelict areas because they cannot afford any place else. People unable to earn enough to keep up with the standards of industrial society have to be helped. The American black from a primitive rural society will require more than one generation of help until his earning ability lets him have a chance in free enterprise. There is no right or reason for a wealthy civilized society in the twentieth century not to apply the full weight of its resources to eradicate its pockets of poverty. But poverty is not eliminated by urban design, nor will the cities renew themselves by eliminating poverty.

Most cities in the United States are desperately fighting urban deterioration with zoning laws, in an effort to stop the process, if not the cause. And the process is important because of the virulence with which deterioration spreads. People demand zoning regulations in order to protect themselves. Zoning laws in most cities are very strict, but on the other hand automatically create privileged urban sites. Changes in zoning become sources of private gain and lead to municipal corruption in the allocation of variances.

The spread of deterioration is in many cases the result of improper invasion of one type of land use by another. At point of contact the land of more intense use paralyzes and dissolves a sector of the other, and as it invades creates a large area of deterioration. Healthy, pleasant towns or suburbs often lose their urban quality in a pattern similar to the following simplified sequence.

Business sectors in American towns have traditionally been separated from residential areas by public or civic buildings, which in most cases are surrounded by ample, pleasant, landscaped spaces. This is true of both small towns and healthy suburbs. As business expands it breaks through this insulation and makes direct contact with the residential areas. Since commercial land is in general more valuable than residential, property owners, real estate agents, businessmen, and merchants frequently approve of the spillage. As a matter of fact, the expansion of business sometimes fills the community with joy as people see their town or suburb "progress."

Business also expands along routes of traffic, even where the routes cut across residential areas. As the commercial area grows, residential property in contact with the land in transformation increases in value as a zone of future business expansion; however, it becomes paralyzed so far as maintenance is concerned, since nobody wants to invest in improving a house that may be removed or remodeled for business. Meanwhile, the area is abandoned by its regular residents, and becomes inexpensive housing often rented by the room to newcomers or low-income groups. When this phase has taken place, the belt around the business section becomes dilapidated and crowded, and usually the slum appears.

A drastic drop in real estate prices then affects the residential part of town in contact with such areas. The drop in prices signifies abundance of property for sale as the people, unhappy with the neighborhood, begin to move out. Another decaying ring is formed. This situation is sometimes made worse by land speculators, who bring commerce or industry into those threatened residential areas to take advantage of low property values or to create an artificial increase in the price of land. When that happens, the process of deterioration is intensified as each of these new spots begins to exercise its own decaying influence. As if weakened by infection, the urban shell shows large areas of dilapidated property or lots which owners prefer to empty buildings for tax reasons or use more profitably for parking lots.

Promoters, attracted to cities in "progress," move rapidly and, over the desks of money-lenders, plan developments on the empty peripheral land. Rural counties are delighted by the prospect of new taxpayers, no zoning, no controls, nobody there to lose, only landowners happy to see farms become urban property. By now, who would possibly want to be close to the center of town, surrounded by unsightly neighborhoods and traffic, looking at dilapidated bars, gas stations, parking lots?

To this positive pressure, which pushes people out, the land promoters and home builders add a pull toward their new developments, picturing in the newspapers lovely mansions under old trees surrounded by open countryside. When the prospective buyer gets to the sales office after driving many miles, he finds the house much smaller than he thought, in a treeless landscape of recently moved earth, squeezed among other houses just like it. When he decides to run away, it is too late. If the promoters have not convinced him with fast talk and double talk, they have already convinced his wife.

The process which creates urban derelict areas is accelerated by the poor quality of those new developments from which people move as fast as they can. Some of those new developments have no quality except being new. With very little money down and easy terms, people move in. As soon as their income improves, they move out in search of better social status in better neighborhoods. What is left is a house that is not new any more. It needs paint and roof repairs. The washing machine and refrigerator are not "automatic." The mortgage has been partially paid, the price of the houses goes down, and so does the neighborhood. Thus the once wholesome town grows rapidly. Very few structures are built in the core. A large zone around the center, and along incoming routes, has become an ugly, semi-commercial, semi-industrial sector, with empty parking lots and big billboards as its only decoration. And behind that, urban derelict areas or slums. Around the city, hundreds of square miles of new developments are scattered where the speculator or the money-lender decided he could make more profit.

New commercial centers with parking facilities appear. New, clean, comfortable structures serve the people living miles away from the original center of town. The suburban commercial center has everything: It is concentrated, has covered pedestrian circulation, air conditioning, soft canned music. The core of the city begins to feel the lack of business, and like the rest of the urban shell, it now begins to deteriorate. The empty parking lot, the hot dog stand, and the gas station creep into what was once valuable commercial property in the core of the city itself.

Urban derelict areas do not generate much in taxes. But large sections of the decaying urban shell, although sparsely occupied, require services and attention. Slums generate more crime and require more public assistance than new suburbs ten times their size in population and tax revenue. Under these conditions the central cities and old suburbs are in a state of financial exhaustion. The remedy applied today is more taxes for those who can pay them, and less service for everybody. As a result, people move even faster to new areas where newer and wealthier municipalities offer more for less.

Since most American cities do not have barriers to their physical extension, reduction in the price of urban land fails to generate demand. Only on very rare occasions is a sector rebuilt by private enterprise. The heavily subsidized Federal urban renewal programs are being applied with very limited results.

As long as there is big and easy money to be made by the urbanization of empty land, the expansion of the cities will continue, subsidized by the taxpayers. It is they who pay for expanded service lines, streets, and urban renewal or other programs to help clean out the derelict areas.

Expanding cities require transportation—automobiles, two or three per family—and automobiles require freeways. Freeways make it possible for people to live even farther away and as the city expands, decay increases in the central areas. To bring people back, more freeways are built. As the freeways criss-cross the city, large areas are severed and killed by these

poorly planned concrete barriers. Still more people move to the outskirts, encouraged by the freeways, which make it possible for them to commute if they wish.

For more than a century cities all over the world adopted the boulevard idea. Enlightened civic leaders, enterprising chambers of commerce, dictators, kings, emperors, all favored boulevards in their cities. It was a local improvement to look forward to and an achievement to be proud of. Today it is freeways. Every progressive town wants its freeway, if possible with a cloverleaf interchange. But boulevards were opened not only as a means of circulation, but to adorn the city with trees and gardens, to provide a place for citizens to walk and enjoy the pleasure of sun and air, and to make an attractive setting for buildings. With boulevards, cities looked more beautiful than ever before. Boulevards drew people to them. Property values were enhanced. In contrast, freeways built today are not decorative, pleasant, or attractive, and do not increase the value of city land they cross.

As planned today, the freeways facilitate circulation to the city or among its distant areas, but cut circulation within and between sectors of the city. In fact, freeways, as planned by engineers today, are doing to the city what railroads did in the last century: cut, divide, kill. All progressive cities are moving railroads out and freeways in. Remove one railroad, build five freeways. But the fact is that freeways are more massive and their power of cutting and dividing will prove to be more deadly.

As a result of the Great Depression of the thirties, people gave the government authority to avoid the repetition of a calamity created by uncontrolled financial speculation. Calamities never happen in the same way, and only fools expect them to. Crazy speculation with empty land has brought to

San Francisco Freeway, by Michael Bry. Used by permission of Michael Bry.

American cities another great depression, and only proper legislation, together with very large sums of government money and emergency programs, will restore the cities to health. This depression is less dramatic because it has happened slowly; but in dollars, cents, and human welfare it is even more tragic than that of the thirties.

It is only in the last few years that the people and their leaders have shown some concern for the American city. The collapse of the old political structure based on the farmers' vote has much to do with it. With the cities holding the large majority and the more vocal population, the political structure of the nation has turned urban. People are becoming concerned with urban problems. Only twenty-five years ago, the majority of Americans or their parents had been born on farms here or in Europe. Their criteria and ideals were rural and agricultural. In the light of these criteria, and of romantic puritanism in the English tradition, the city was considered inherently ugly, unhealthy, and immoral.

Because of the common language, England has always had great influence on the thinking of the United States. What was said in England during the last century about mining towns and industrial slums was absorbed in the United States as if the coal mines were those of Pennsylvania and Pennsylvania were half the country. In fact the social problems and human situations portrayed by Dickens rarely existed in the United States, and of course had a totally different character. But so many novels and so many poets said so much on the same theme that in the end they created in the United States, already sensitive on the subject, a strong prejudice against cities. The result was an obsession with the small community as a savior of mankind and the garden suburb as its substitute.

It greatly contributed to the disregard by Congress of the welfare of the American city.

Nineteenth-century English economic pragmatism found its perfect expression in the concept that what is not good business does not deserve attention. The supposition that if people wanted better cities they would have had them by now has become part of the political and business philosophy of most American leaders. But the people do not demand better cities because the choice has never been offered. People generally accept as immutable what they find when they are born and what they grow up with. They cannot imagine anything else. People appreciate the beauty of small New England towns, but do not want to live in New England towns. People who travel admire the charm and elegance of some European cities, but do not want to live in European cities. So far as the American city is concerned, they feel there is no alternative: it has to be the amorphous, garish, provisional thing it is. When knowledgeable and sensitive people have pointed out the unnecessary flaws in the American city, they have elicited great response and enthusiasm from those people who were already concerned. The average citizen is simply not interested. The general problems of the city have always been beyond his understanding. To him urban problems are the minuscule problems of his neighborhood.

The new urban society will have to understand what the city is and what it could be. The basic knowledge should be taught from elementary school on, for the urban environment is to man what the pond is to the fish. What could be more important? No wonder the Greeks felt that virtue and honor in a man were to be measured by the well-being and beauty he could bring to his city.

Concern for the American city has been shallow and partial until now. Only two points of view have made themselves heard. One is the social approach, strong because it has political appeal. This approach tends to transform city problems into problems of "poverty" and suggests that it is possible to create great cities by abolishing poverty, disease, and crime; in other words, by eradicating symptoms. To approach the city from the "poverty" point of view is like approaching the understanding of man from the disease point of view. It is partial, to say the least.

The second theory claims that the city is ugly and should be made beautiful. This initiative has had very little effect. Solutions proposed have been mostly on the cosmetic side and people have rightly understood the campaign for the beautification of the cities as a great program for "urban decoration." Pain and ugliness are warnings. To destroy pain or ugliness without dealing with the cause is not only useless, it is irrational.

Cities have been the physical containers for the societies of men. These societies are very new and are in a period of formation, but with the help of the human brain, they are rapidly becoming more complex and developed. The sickness or health of human societies will henceforth largely depend on the ability of human beings to create their proper physical container.

The human body is a very complicated container in which a galaxy of societies of living elements exists in ideal media under ideal conditions. Health in man depends on maintaining these conditions inside and finding the proper conditions outside. Until recently people had primitive ideas about the functioning of the human body, probably just as primitive as our present concept of human society.

If man is considered to be one million years old, more or less, it was only in the last one-quarter of one percent of this time span, in the fifth century before Christ, that Hippocrates achieved an incomplete but fairly accurate concept of what a human body is. Only five hundred years ago, knowledge of man's body was not better than when it was explained by Galen, another Greek, in the second century B.C. And not until the seventeenth century, when the cell was discovered, was there even the suspicion that men were made of societies of microscopic living organisms.

Only 330 years ago, Descartes, one of the most brilliant minds in history, stated that all human thinking could be worked out in terms of mathematical reasoning, which makes him a grandfather of the modern computer. On the other hand, such a materialistic interpretation of man's superior brain could not conceive the unity of body and soul. To him, the human body was the mechanical container of the soul. As if to prove it, he built incredibly sophisticated mechanical dolls that could walk and dance.

From the earliest times, man observed that sickness of the body created dullness and sometimes brightness of the spirit. The reverse process, although clearly observable, was almost always either denied or moved into the category of the supernatural. There are many records, mostly of a religious kind, of cures as the result of the influence of a strong mind on a receptive spirit. Hypnosis became popular in Europe at the end of the nineteenth century. Charcot in Paris was able to create artificial symptoms of disease in a patient under hypnosis and to remove painful symptoms from a sick body.

It was only in the present century, however, that an attempt was made to unify scientifically, in a single concept, body mechanism, sensations, and behavior. Freud demonstrated that the body's mechanism affected the emotions and that those emotions affected the body mechanism. Probably his most important contribution to the knowledge and understanding of man was his demonstration of a direct relationship between man as a unity of societies and the outside universe which man perceives and understands through the delicate and sensitive mechanism of the mind. He showed how physical health and spiritual happiness depend on a harmony between the two, while disharmony and conflict create disease and spiritual misery. His basic thought was that neurosis is

By Federico García Lorca. Reprinted from *Poeta en Nueva York,* by F. G. Lorca, by permission of Francisco García Lorca.

an unresolved conflict between the individual and an external influence. With psychoanalysis Freud was able to perform cures on hysterical subjects who were suffering from blindness, paralysis and other physical disabilities.

General medicine progressed on a separate but parallel path. As new tools and techniques of observation were invented, it became possible to prove scientifically what was already popular knowledge: the everyday interrelation of the functioning of the human organism and external influences. For instance, a malfunctioning of the stomach or the liver can cause moods of depression affecting outlook on the world, and external conditions which create feelings of depression affect the working of the body and often produce malfunctioning of the digestive system.

Psychology had also progressed in the same direction since the beginning of the century when Pavlov made dogs secrete digestive juices at the sound of a bell. Observation of human reflex actions and reactions built a useful pragmatic science which demonstrated the close relationship of body functioning to exterior physical conditions. The influence of exterior physical conditions on the behavior of groups of people has always been recognized. It was well known that dirty places induced people to throw trash on them, and impeccable places made people check on their own neatness. Since this kind of observation, although very real, could not be counted or measured, it belonged to the field of mass psychology, a vague and undetermined science.

Fortunately, the concept of statistics, which already existed in the minds of a few Frenchmen and Englishmen of the eighteenth century, became important with the advent of industrialization and mass production. The punctured card an engineer had invented in France at the beginning of the

eighteenth century to make patterns in mechanically produced textiles, became very handy in statistics. With statistics,
mass psychology and social behavior became a science. It was
then possible to measure the effect that an environment had
on people. Some of the first observations, made in factories,
proved that neat quiet working space induced a certain percentage of workers to be more careful, with the result that the
number of mistakes and the rate of accidents were lowered
in a certain percentage. From that time on the trend was initiated toward scientific improvement in the working environment of man, making it possible for people to perform better
with better light, sound control, and proper temperature. It
has proceeded in the last few years to the introduction of music, special colors, and the like. Today it is considered important for good performance of the personnel in an office that
the place be clean, the desks in good order, the light intensity
and the level of sound adequate, and the temperature comfortable. Only half a century ago, this would have been considered useless luxury, unimportant, or even harmful pamper-
ing. It was only in this century that man acquired a concept of
health, bodily, mental and spiritual health, not as the nega-
tion of disease, but from the positive point of view of general
well-being.

But the influence of the environment affects not only the
individual's comfort and performance. We have recently
learned that it affects the health of society. One of the most
interesting discoveries of our time has come from the methodical observation of animals in their natural habitat. New
studies have revealed the enormous importance of the physical environment in the social behavior of animals, especially
the more intelligent ones. Thanks to the patience and dedication of people who have gained the animals' confidence and

lived with them, or who have observed their habits for a long period of time from inconspicuous places, it is known today that individual behavior depends far more than previously assumed on the quality of social organization, and that the quality of social organization depends directly on the physical environment.

This discovery is important not only because it has taught man a great deal about his cousins, but because the incomplete and inadequate observation of animals in zoos, made after Darwin's discoveries and hypotheses, had created misunderstandings which influenced our concepts of human behavior. Darwin's theory of evolution and progress was, if not based on, at least influenced by Adam Smith's theory of free enterprise. Profit in nature became sex and food, for which all animals were competing. The strongest simply ate more, became stronger, beat their competitors, had more females, and reared more babies. As a result, there were better and better specimens in each generation. A corollary of this principle is that the best is the one that takes the most. Another conclusion is that sex and food are what everybody competes for. In man this means money, since money can buy sex and food.

The popular interpretation of great thinkers has always been wrong. Darwin was an extremely sensitive individual and often stated his fears that simplification of his concepts could bring error. The term "survival of the fittest," which he borrowed from Herbert Spencer, meant more than "me first." But Darwin also lived and published his most famous books in the middle of the nineteenth century, when man's understanding of nature and its ecology was rather primitive. That many of his assumptions were later proved inaccurate does not detract from his genius, which put together a logical and unified explanation of the mechanisms of nature, any more than Columbus' unawareness of having discovered a new continent detracts from his extraordinary accomplishment.

The basic drives of life are to preserve itself and to reproduce itself. But we know today that the process is not simple. Animals are not necessarily happy when provided with comfort, plenty of food, and healthy young females. Life does not work like the machine the nineteenth century thought it was. In captivity, all individuals of some species and some individuals of others simply stop eating and die. In certain cases, the animals seem to be healthy and gain weight, but are not interested in sex, and the zoo has to maintain stock by acquiring new specimens. Many animals simply do not reproduce in captivity. The more intelligent animals have more chance of survival and reproduction in captivity, for their adaptability is greater, but their instincts frequently become perverted: males abuse females and kill them, males fight and kill one another, males and females kill, and in some cases, eat their babies. Abandoning of newborn by females is a frequent occurrence.

Obviously something very important is missing for the animal in the zoo. Until very recently the answer was simple: "freedom," an answer in existence for many centuries but packaged and labeled in the eighteenth century: Nature is free. The birds fly in the blue sky singing the happiness of freedom. The butterflies, with their bright colors, move with the freedom of the wind, and the fish swim over the immense freedom of the ocean.

"Animals want to be free, but if they were free, we would not have a zoo," says the zoo keeper. Better and larger cages with rocks made of concrete in imitation of the natural environment were built, in an effort to "fool the animals." Captive animals have been happier since these fundamental improvements which help the less intelligent ones gain a degree or two in the scale of adaptation. Today it is beginning to be understood that animals in captivity, including domestic animals, do not behave like their wild brothers because the inadequate artificial environment disturbs the social mechanisms. The zoo may in some cases be an acceptable habitat for the individual, but it is unsuitable for the healthy performance of the individual as part of the species. Once social responsibility breaks down, the individual disobeys the natural laws of social behavior and even those of self-preservation. We know today that wild animals are not free, that their social organization is very strict, that their taboos are many, and that their *esprit de corps* may reach the point of heroism.

Animals in general, but especially the more developed ones, when in the natural environment, rarely kill except to eat. Fighting to the death among members of one species for food or sexual conquest is very rare as a social practice. Animals' concept of territory is so strong that the individual is ready to risk his life in defense of the social property. Social hierarchy is so strict and defined among many fishes, birds, and most mammals, that there are no two individuals of the group in the same category. There is a continuous struggle for position in a hierarchy that brings better rights within the community, not usually achieved through fights, but rather through a balance of challenges not yet well understood. Hierarchy implies rank, and high rank more rights and duties, which together generate responsibility.

The process of selection of mates is a ritual in which many complicated forces are involved. Females like to be close to power, and in most superior species, including man, it is not the female that attracts the male, but the male that attracts the female, with beauty and power. But power in nature is not based on the kind of force that subjugates and ravages. In nature, the leader leads not because he takes the most and piles it up for his own use, but because he is able to offer the most, even to the point of self-sacrifice. In animals (or men) the great takers are those who feel weak and insecure, want to have every kind of protection, and in their fear, pile food and objects up around them even at the cost of their own well-being. The true leader is free and strong and does not need protection. In his wisdom and strength he can give all.

Social organization is the method which nature has from the beginning found to be most efficient for the preservation and multiplication of life. Man himself is the most complicated social organization of social organizations. Man's highly developed brain made it possible for him to create and live in an artificial environment, the city, without serious damage to his social mechanism. For ten thousand years he has been living in urban environments, and the benefits of the interchange of experiences and ideas with other men have proved to be so stimulating that man has thrived and his accomplishments have increased in tempo, quality, and scope.

Only in the last 150 years have conditions in cities deteriorated as a proper human habitat and only in the last thirty have some of them become unsuitable. The vast and sudden increase in population has created a gigantic concentration in cities meant for another density. Industry has invaded the city intended for another use. Automobiles, mass-produced, flood streets unsuitable for them, and add noise and confusion. Pollution of the air and water by industrial plants, plus the tension generated by industry as it pumps its products through high-pressure advertising, have destroyed the environment man requires for the proper functioning of his social mechanism. He is showing some of the symptoms of the animal in the zoo.

It is common in our time to measure man's social progress in terms of food consumption, health, and longevity. Animals in zoos are well-kept and fed and, when adapted to their routine of captivity, are apparently healthier and live longer than wild ones. That the more intelligent ones spend their lives pacing their cages in eternal hope of escape speaks for itself.

Man's life in many of the large industrial cities crawls by in an atmosphere of routine and frustration. Tension, hate, and sadness have distorted the faces of the people riding on subways or waiting in the large bus and railway stations of the world. Crime is common and perversion abundant, barely kept in check or forced underground by the police who in large, advanced societies have become very large and very advanced in their systems of watching over the behavior of individuals and punishing the ones at fault with isolation or death. The law, the government, the job, the standards of behavior, have created the cages within which most people spend their lives monotonously pacing from one side to the other, getting fat, living longer, and saving money in hope of escape.

Industrialized modern societies are proud of offering people opportunity. Opportunity has become the equivalent of social and moral justice. Opportunity has also become synonymous with change, for we have come to believe that everybody is unhappy, or at least should be. Those hundreds of millions of dollars invested in advertising that feeds on frustration do not go to waste. Women try desperately to stop time. Men hate their jobs and feel humiliated by their performance in life. Ambitions beyond means, hopes beyond possibilities. Disruption of the basic principle of cause and effect.

The present is a time of rapid physical progress. In a healthy society this means a happy climate of opportunity. A healthy society is recognized by the intelligent pride each individual takes in what he is and what he does. In a healthy group, age is a characteristic that engenders respect because the individuals grow to be worthy of respect, each one on his own terms. In a healthy society the success of one individual is reason for general pride and joy. In the unhealthy milieu of the large industrial cities of today, anxiety and hate are sometimes the only moral and intellectual stimulus. Individual and social crime are twice as common, statistics say, as they were thirty years ago and three times what they still are in rural towns; crime as the result of extreme dissatisfaction, pathological ambition, or paranoid schizophrenia too abundant to be institutionalized. Insanity is an involuntary refuge. Alcohol, marijuana, morphine, cocaine, and LSD are voluntary shelters or escapes.

In a medium of frustration man hates success in others, and takes for granted that others hate him in success. This obsession has become a persecution complex in which whole nations grow to believe that they are hated because they are successful, and in their mania create wars they believe to be in self-defense.

Two centuries ago some people thought there was no crime in the wild and that the savage state was the ideal for man. Rousseau created a sensation with this theory in the France of the eighteenth century, where artificiality had become prevalent in the era of wigs and crinolines and the *philosophes* delighted themselves with the idea of man's "mastery of nature." Rousseau has had many followers since who, like Gauguin, abandoned the sophisticated city in search of the ideal free environment. The question is which is the real primitive environment? For some it would be the primeval jungle of New Guinea; for others, idyllic Tahiti. To others it is the simple biblical setting of Judea, extremely sophisticated, of course, compared to New Guinea, or the lovely dusty roads with lacy willows and ox-carts of India, or the little village in the Alps. Which is the true free society in which man can be at his best? Athens? Florence? Paris of the last century? New York today? Judging by the eagerness with which man is absorbing the industrial and scientific era, chances are that he will move fast toward a society far more complex than the present. This suggests that man is now in a primitive state to which some unhappy inhabitant of the future will surely want to escape, calling it an ideal free society.

Some people believe the best environment for man is nature in its most "natural" state. They think ecology suffers every time man constructs anything, for by doing so, he destroys the perfect natural equilibrium. These are the people who get up every morning only to learn from the newspapers that the world is going the wrong way. They think total happiness is to be totally surrounded by nature, like a cow in a meadow. But the Athens of Pericles was artificial and so was Florence of the 1500's. There was more intelligent thought and more sensitive creativity in those cities in one day than in all the lovely wilderness of the world in history.

Permanent solutions have never been based on escape, on going back, but only on moving ahead. The urban problems of today are not going to be solved by imitating the wilderness, the farm, or the small village, for although the present city is an unhappy place, it attracts people from woods, farms, and small villages where there are other more confining cages that also imprison man. Man and his social organization are being hurt by the conditions of the city today, yet at the same time, man is being stimulated by the large social congregation.

Progress in evolution has always been toward unification, unification in the organized living cell, in the society of cells, in the society of societies of cells. On the other hand, the first element of life appeared only when the proper environment was ready. Every effort since has been to maintain the ideal physical environment artificially in more and more complicated organisms and finally in man, himself a universe in which the ideal physical and chemical environment is sustained artificially for each one of his cells. This by no means implies that nature has copied the original environmental media. Nature has rather re-created ideal conditions in an artificial way, similar to that in which man has created modern agriculture. In the urban environment as in the vineyard or orchard if the habitat shows signs of disease and deterioration, the solution is not to return to primitive systems, but to move to more advanced ones.

It is not true that to gain the benefits of congregation and interchange, man has to pay a price in happiness and social health. With a proper understanding of nature and a proper knowledge of man and his societies, it will be possible to create a healthy, pleasant, stimulating urban environment, using newly discovered and almost unlimited sources of materials and energy. Before many years, perhaps by the next century, the concepts of rural and urban population will not exist. The people of the earth will be totally urbanized, with only a few living on farms, of no more importance than the small segment of the population that today lives around mines.

The present is a time of great vitality. Man's appetite for understanding has reached heights never imagined. Man's curiosity is taking him deep into the mysterious unknown regions of the origins of life, the structure of the atom, and the composition and dimensions of the universe. If the Renaissance was the epoch of the discovery of space perspective and the obsession with the third dimension, ours is the era of creativity with the dimension and perspective of time. Our world is truly a new world. Unfortunately our feelings and sometimes our thinking are still far behind. We still separate nature from man. Although we know that life requires a medium for its proper development, that plants die or degenerate when placed in inadequate conditions of light, humidity, temperature, and air, that animals in an improper environment suffer harm to their social structure with ill effects to the individuals, we seem to believe that man is beyond all that. Our eighteenth-century rationalism still believes these problems are moral and have moral social solutions; our petulant nineteenth-century romanticism still finds spiritual causes.

Man, like any other animal, will find peace, security, and happiness only in a habitat that stimulates his social responsibility. As in the animal world, the conditions which produce this habitat are physical, and must not violate the ancestral ties between man and nature. It was only yesterday in the long history of man that children grew up surrounded by nature's products: trees, plants, grass, flowers, sea, rivers, mountains, cows, horses, worms. Men's eyes, ears, hands, and brain were molded by living among nature's deeds. Nature has unity, for each thing has affected another in the history of its development, and is still affecting it. The color of the tree affects the color of the ground and the colors of both affect us.

Sound is always in the air when we are surrounded by nature. It comes very much like color on a well-measured scale.

The sounds of the wind, the rain, and the sea are large in quantity and soft in quality, pierced by the short high-pitched sounds of birds and insects. Because screaming usually implies extreme emotion, our automatic mechanisms react instantly. And we react automatically to an infinite number of combinations of light with sound, sound with texture, color with flavor, and so on. This is the world that made us: we are part of it.

Nature has scale: there are big things like the ocean or the sky, and little things like leaves, insects, and children's fingers. The ocean and the sky have one kind of proportion, flowers have another. We belong to the universal scale of proportions. Man's sensory system and automatic reactions are and for thousands of years will be essentially the same as those of the man who lived 100,000 years ago. They were built by a painful process of billions of years of evolution and are not going to change in any appreciable way in a few years, or centuries.

In the United States, where the proportion of farm population is today one of the smallest in the world, the majority of the people lived in a rural environment until only a generation ago. Today only ten percent of the children do, although many city suburbs are somewhat rural in character. Children live today mostly in a world of man-made things: streets, buildings, machines, furniture, and toys. This is a new world, the world in which they and future generations will live.

Time is one of the dimensions of nature. Time is change. Without change there is no life. To stop change is to stop existence. As the physical world changed in its evolution, some regions of the earth became unsuitable for man, and he moved. When modern man finds his physical environment unsuitable, he changes the environment. Man is in urgent need of changing it now. Man's receptive mechanism is being hurt by the lack of harmony and proportion in the scale, form, texture, color, and sound of his improvised artificial industrial environment. Our task, now that the human population of the earth is going to live surrounded by man-made things, is to adapt those things to man's perceptive mechanism, and not the other way around.

The discovery of the direct relationship between environment and social behavior, and its impact on the sense of responsibility and happiness of the individual, is the most fascinating new horizon of our time. Its study we call *ambiology*. Understanding it is probably the most important of present human tasks.

Since the beginning of time, and today among primitive tribes, men have painted their faces, tattooed their bodies, decorated their temples, and adorned their tools and weapons. In fact, many of these artificial ornamentations became the distinction between classes, making hierarchies visible: drab for the slave, most elaborate for the king, and no effort enough to please the gods' insatiable appetite for beauty. This pattern, with small variations, has existed and will continue to exist in every human society. Although at present, men in Western cultures do not paint their faces (not very much), do not have slaves (not really), and there are very few kings left; on the other hand, industry and affluence have built temples to many more idols and have multiplied tools and weapons by the millions.

Nature has also been visually conscious for billions of years. In nature, hierarchies are also expressed in terms of beauty. Living things have been aesthetically conscious since the beginning or almost the beginning of life. Among most developed types of life, animal or vegetable, the healthier and stronger show their qualities not only in size but in their colors or in the elegance with which they stand or move.

Disease is ugly. Where there is something missing, there is ugliness. Scarcity is ugly. The animal with falling hair or the plant with sick leaves is ugly. We have learned from nature to recognize health or excellence by what we call beauty. In fact, we know today that in most animals this is one of the criteria by which the female picks the male, and therefore that aesthetics is one of the most important directional systems nature uses for the development of species. It is not that the strongest male kills or keeps the competition away by force so that he can have females in quantity. It is not that the females measure the territory of each prospective mate and decide on the basis of wealth and security either. The selection of mates is not that simple. What makes certain specimens attractive is a combination of many qualities. Those qualities usually express themselves physically.

To become a leader, to become the head of a large group, an animal must exhibit many attributes in the right formula. Sometimes in our complicated modern society, we think the president is the one in the center of the picture, who turns out to be the chauffeur or the bodyguard, but most of the time it is clear who is who: among animals, because nature makes it obvious, and among men, because nature, with the help of the human brain, takes care of that also. The king of the tribe or of a civilized country, the witch doctor or the high priest, the head of the warriors or the general, are easily distinguishable: more feathers, more bright colors, and more medals. And when facts do not coincide with the physical representation he is supposed to have, the popular imagination or local artist will make the king, the high priest, or the general, bigger and more brightly colored.

The farmer speaks about beautiful cows, or crops, the carpenter about a beautiful piece of wood and the real estate man about a beautiful piece of property. What they all imply is high quality. Of course, beauty is relative, and the beautiful airplane of yesterday seems clumsy today. The same is true

The Nyimi, Head of the Bushongo, from *The Sculpture of Africa*, by Eliot Elisofon, and reprinted by permission of the author.

of a dress, a building, an adding machine, and it is true of a bull. The beautiful longhorn of yesterday looks funny now. Whether he also looks funny to the cow is something we do not know. But animals change in their likings too, since that is one of the tools of evolution.

Aesthetics in nature creates the incentive to move in a general direction, while pain and pleasure define the specific direction of the action. Aesthetics corresponds to an alternative road between beauty and ugliness affecting in separate ways man or bee, or amoeba. We are conditioned to look for and to find the maximum degree of beauty when the desired qualities are present in optimum proportion. Ugliness in nature is a warning—it implies disharmony, lack of proportion, wrong functioning, and it means "Stop; change direction."

Conscious aesthetic discernment, the ability to recognize the ugly and the beautiful, per se, is not a common quality. Like the clear recognition of truth or untruth, it is a rare product of cultural sophistication. There are no rules for beauty or truth, for they change in time and space. They do not exist in themselves, for they are relations in the continuous evolution of life and events. Excellence in beauty and the optimum in truth are unpopular because they are always new, they are always pioneering: by the time the majority gets there, facts have made truth and beauty change.

Thought alone has not given us the path to follow. Probably more important has been the instinctive search for harmony in things, relations, and conditions, as felt and perceived by sensitive leaders. For just as the farmer finds beauty in the cow that has the qualities he is after, so does the mathematician in certain numbers and relations, the physicist in concepts, and the statesman in the conditions in a nation.

Creative intuition is, of course, a quality that has to be fed with personal experience or with ideas, spoken, written, or graphically expressed, digested into concepts and molded by the characteristics of each individual. When a concept we have built vibrates on the same frequency as something in nature, whether interior or exterior to man, there is a flood of communication as a specific pool of relations held by nature is released. Here lies the source of great creativity.

A masterpiece of design, a bridge for instance, is not conceived by an engineer who, having learned formulas and systems of handling wood, concrete or steel, applies them in the most intelligent manner. It is conceived through intuition of the way materials can be organized to work harmoniously within the conditions of location, function, climate, economics, etc. These factors, together with many undefinables, crystallize in man's mind in the form of the object. Scientific research enters at this point. Patient work and study confirm, modify, or destroy the concept.

Men have created objects of all kinds; at the beginning, simple tools and weapons made of wood or bones, and later of metals. As civilization developed, tools became more complicated, and in our time they have become very intricate machines. So have weapons. From the beginning, the makers of tools and weapons have given these objects form and color. When men were able to master the production of iron spears or breathtaking jet airplanes, the excellence of these products expressed themselves visually. Men did what nature had done with the tree or the panther. Of course, this kind of creativity requires not only physical dexterity but the intellectual and spiritual wealth the maker gives to the object, for nobody can create anything better than he is. The product then becomes a work of art that communicates its purpose, physically, intellectually, and culturally.

If a particular sword from the time of Charlemagne was a masterpiece, it was because its blade had the best steel, its handle made the holder feel strong and the total was pleasant to the eye because its proportions were in the best human scale. The precious stones and engravings spoke of the owner's feeling of love for it, since only on a very dear friend would such care and wealth be bestowed. At different times in history, people had given this or similar qualities to drinking cups, buildings, boats, or pins to hold their hair. This process by which objects are given intrinsic and intimate human values is art.

Man and some animals, whether or not conscious of the relationship between quality and beauty, have played with beauty in order to create a semblance of quality. This reverse process is very clear in some fishes, birds, and insects, and is true of some plants. Ornamentation with intricate designs and colors can represent false pretenses of quality that serve purposes such as attracting the opposite sex or keeping enemies away. Man has gone far beyond such simple purposes, creating almost a language which by the juxtaposition of positive and negative aesthetic values communicates perceptions in a way similar to that of nature. This too is called art, and explains the confusion that exists as to what is beauty and what is art.

From the time man painted on the walls of caves, he has had the need and felt the urge to communicate experiences and feelings which could not be expressed in words. Painting is a primitive way of communicating ideas but a direct way of expressing perceptions without going through the long sterilizing channels of words. In churches and palaces for 5,000 years artists interpreted with a language of aesthetics what priests and kings wanted to communicate to the people.

Buildings, especially in the past, had a meaning beyond their direct function, and that meaning was reinforced by paintings or sculptures applied to the structure. Sculpture was at one time as essential to the temple or palace as the walls, columns, or roof and in many cases was intimately combined with them. It was common to all civilizations and places from prehistoric China to Mayan Mexico and from the Egyptian civilization to medieval France.

After the dark years brought to Europe by the oriental nihilism which accompanied Christianity, the Italian Renaissance arrived with men exuberant in their desire to create and insatiable in their desire to know and to understand. Because of their better comprehension of nature and man, Renaissance man made spiritual contact with the great Greek and Roman minds through their artistic creations as they were dug from ruins. The high spiritual content of the past was released in the hands of the newly enlightened people of fifteenth-century Italy. It was then that men initiated the custom of keeping close to them at least a piece of those objects to remind them constantly of their incredibly rich message. These objects from the past became scarce as too many people wanted heads of statues, cornices of buildings, amphoras, or even articles which, having been underground for many years, were barely recognizable.

The fifteenth century was the time of commerce. Trading made some people in some Italian cities very rich. The wealthiest began to accumulate these kinds of objects in great quantities, and soon powerful kings all over Europe began to consider them part of the bounty in their wars. Later when the kings lost power, the people took possession of their treasures. This is the origin of most of our present-day museums. When those statues, paintings, columns, or mosaics were taken from their original location they lost most of their intrinsic value. Like words taken out of phrase, their meaning became diffused and their power limited. Museums became big dictionaries in which words were collected. Big and small words out of context. The knowledge of history, geography, and anthropology of a king or wealthy man three hundred years ago was probably inferior in quantity and quality to that of our fifteen-year-olds. This is shown clearly by the British Museum, the Louvre, or Museo Vaticano. They are big collections mostly of junk which with time have become precious like great-grandmother's quilt, things nobody dares to throw away only because they are antiques.

The separation between archaeology and art was not very clear then and in some areas is not very clear today. The Tut-Ankh-Amen treasures, for instance, are both. Today museums have become very useful places where men interested in a scientific approach to history find these "pieces" conveniently concentrated in a few locations.

The unrestricted admiration of the past, at least in recent history, started in the Renaissance and continued for several centuries. It did not stop in collecting, but went on to copying Greek and Roman works of art. Only in the second part of the twentieth century has enthusiasm for Greek and Roman architecture subsided enough to allow the soup factories and radio stations of the most industrialized countries to look like something other than religious temples of 500 B.C. (Many still do.)

The artist of the Renaissance worked for the rich and powerful and indirectly for their collections. Part of the king's collection might have been a beautiful sword handle or the foot of a statue. These objects in time became more and more precious and were shown like jewels, sometimes in velvet boxes. When artists began to produce for the collectors, they began to create handles without swords and feet without statues.

When very few people knew how to read or write, among other reasons because there were very few books, painting was one of the most important means of mass communication. The Church used paintings to communicate its teachings to masses of illiterate people. During the early Renaissance, when commerce made some of the Italian cities rich in money and ideas, painting blazed with light and warmth that have reached our time: Giotto, Fra Angelico, Botticelli, express in an almost magical way the meeting of the two main cultures of East and West, of Byzantium and Italy, and two epochs, the Middle Ages and the Renaissance. Michelangelo and Leonardo da Vinci reflect in their work the brilliance of the Renaissance with its love of form, light, perspective, passionate interest in the appearance and workings of the human body, and intellectual approach to mystic and religious themes.

Toward the end of the Renaissance, when oil painting techniques became widely known and more people could afford pictures, hundreds of artists did portraits of noblemen and handsome overdressed or underdressed ladies. Later, as the great movement toward nature took place in France, there were portraits of nature, cows grazing, misty countrysides, ladies in love with horses or angels, or dead ducks lying on tables, surrounded by apples. In more recent times, as goods became more abundant and there were more rich merchants and more artists, paintings became a commodity, merchandise that could be placed anywhere, portable culture.

Photography was invented in 1826 by Daguerre, a French painter. Soon afterwards, it was possible for anybody to own "art" masterpieces of exact reproduction. Landscapes with very fine cows and pretty reclining nudes became available in detailed reproductions at very reasonable prices. Then came cinematography. How could a simple mode of expression like painting compete in the artificial art of communicating perceptions with cinema which not only has more possibilities of light, but also the dimension of time?

Painters at the end of the last century were faced with the extinction of their art. In a superb effort they began to look for new and untouched areas and thereby produced one of the most creative and exciting periods in the history of painting. The task was first to destroy, to clean from the minds of people the useless cluttered accumulation of clichés. To get to the sensitive parts of the soul it was necessary to penetrate the crust of prejudice. If photography was accurate, their paintings made a point of being inaccurate. There was unlimited experimentation with color used differently from the way nature does—green skies, blue trees. Shadows applied on the wrong side or on both sides of an object, independent of the light sources. Primary colors. Complicated colors made of the combination of many dots. Superimposition of forms. New forms. Combinations of shocking elements: a guitar in a landscape of triangles. Expeditions into the world of the subconscious. Expeditions into social and political fields. The world of insects and microbes. The internal organs. The celestial bodies in landscapes of infinity. Experiments with the forms of new machines, mass production expressed in stereotyped objects. Rediscovery of the primitive. Expression through forms and symbols borrowed from Africa's past and present. Japan. The Eskimos. Experimentation in portraying sex physically and intellectually. Use of the ugly and the unpleasant as graphic values. Great interest in the absurd. Then came ab-

straction, abstraction that became a *tour de force* in the decoration of canvases, decoration or anti-decoration. Pop art, op
art, and other kinds of art followed. At that point painting
began to use burned mattresses.

The painter, like a bird caught inside a room, has exhausted himself and now flutters in a corner with less and
less vitality. He has very little more to say and nowhere to
go. This period, which extends into our time, has exhausted
almost every approach, every technique, every subject.

Sculpture has experienced a similarly painful process, although without the vitality and brilliance of painting. Today
both media, exhausted, interchange means of expression.
Sometimes painting is three dimensional and sculpture is flat.
Their survival today is in the hands of the museums and private collectors.

The sudden and surprising course that painting took in
France at the turn of the century, and later on in the rest of
the world, caused a few great painters to pass undetected for
some time. When later they were recognized, demand for
their work was so sudden, so great, and by such a wealthy
group, that prices of some canvases increased a thousand
times in a few years. Today there are many people hoping for
this to happen again and again with every unrecognized painter or sculptor, a situation which of course stimulates demand
and production, and supports the art galleries. During the
centuries in which this production of museum art has taken
place, people continued to make tools and weapons: chairs,
musical instruments, automobiles, airplanes, adding machines, rockets, and millions of other objects.

The artistic achievements of an epoch have been, and still
are, measured by those objects that specifically belong to that
epoch and express that specific culture. Greek statuary and

temples were an intrinsic part of Greek life. The same can be said of the Gothic cathedral in relation to the Middle Ages. The magnificent religious paintings of the Italian pre-Renaissance were painted to communicate peace, tenderness, mystic feelings, sorrow, to the common man and were a function of the needs of that specific time. Today art in the United States and in the Western world in general is still measured by nineteenth-century European standards. Opera, ballet, symphonic concerts, theater, painting, sculpture, are all great cultural expressions of the post-Renaissance agricultural society that reached its climax in Europe during the nineteenth century, when wealth from colonial possessions and profits from industry became available to the arts.

Rich industrialists in the United States still play the worn-out game of great patron of the arts in the best Renaissance style, and collect what the art critics point out as valuable, without realizing not only that the stage has changed, but that the audience is gone. It is unfortunate that they are not interested in the design quality of neon signs, gas stations, lunch counters, or television programs, products that belong to our time and correspond to the intrinsic culture of industrial America at the middle and end of the twentieth century. If in the future the present American civilization is rediscovered, it will be the automobile wheels, typewriters, plastic containers, and video tapes which men will keep in their historical "art" museums. And as with the Mayas, Greeks, Romans, or with the Italians of the *Cinquecento*, civilization will be judged by the man-made things among which we live, of which the largest and most important are, of course, our cities.

The universe intercommunicates. Nature intercommunicates. The human body is an intricate and complicated society of societies, whose functioning depends upon immediate and accurate intercommunication among its parts. Animals intercommunicate. Social animals are those which have achieved better intercommunication. Men created cities in order to achieve easier intercommunication. Civilization is the result of man's ability to intercommunicate ideas and share experiences. Primitive languages or geographical barriers which have prevented people from intercommunicating properly have kept those societies in primitive stages of cultural development.

Intercommunication combines ideas and works something like this:

> A by itself is only A.
> A and B can be A + B or B + A or AB or BA or A–B or
>   A   B
> B–A or B or A and so on.

A, B, and C already make the number of combinations quite sizable. The combination of ideas works differently from a combination of simple letters or numbers, since ideas contain qualitative values. Earth + Bird creates an infinite number of possibilities, for both elements are innumerable in their interpretations. Man finds more and more meanings as he discovers and understands more and more of the surrounding universe.

Words are mostly ideas or idea-connectors. Language is an orderly expression of ideas, limited in time by the speed of the tongue when talking, the hand when writing, or the eye when reading. Concepts are groups of ideas and feelings, digested, integrated, and organized into units by the human brain. As men interchange ideas, the scope of thought increases in geometric proportion and concept-building is stimulated in an even larger proportion.

We think in words, sentences, phrases. Thinking parallels language in form and speed. The power of the brain is consequently ill-used and wasted by our need to express ideas in words, and by the fact that words define and limit ideas.

Speaking and writing are "intellectual" communication. A written explanation of a glass of water to somebody who has never experienced one, a creature from another planet, for instance, would become a book of thousands of pages and still would not really explain the essence of glass, of weight, of light, and still less, the intimate feeling of thirst and the other experienced relations of water with the human body. On the other hand, the brain can combine a glass of water with tennis and friends in a fraction of a second, although both tennis and friends would also require millions of words.

A present-day computer can perform more than a million operations per second, and soon may reach a billion. The brain has about 10,000 times as many components as a large contemporary computer. Although the time reaction for a neuron, which is the basic unit of the brain, is 1,000 times slower than that of an electron, the computer component, the brain has a much higher efficiency because it uses many chains

"The Conversation Lags," from *All Embarrassed*, by William Steig. Reprinted by permission of the author.

of components at the same time in parallel lines, while the computer uses them in succession. Our brain performs as a massive team of computers. (Massive indeed: each cell may connect with 10,000 others. The most complex computer unit connects in no more than five or six different ways.) Moreover, the neuron is a living cell, subject to the reactions and mutations of a living organism. And although the mental process is basically an electromagnetic process, the elements are not stable. The neurons are in continuous change. The sensory impressions originated in the eyes, mouth, ears, nose, or skin, or an infinite number of other interior and exterior sources of sensations, stimulate gland secretions that modify the blood, the neuron, and ultimately thought. The process can also be reversed; that is, an idea can create a chemical chain reaction that will affect the senses and modify their perception and information, and so on.

This does not mean that the brain can always perform better than the computer. In very narrow, specific directions, the computer's thought-process can be as dramatically efficient compared to the human brain as a modern aircraft compared to a man walking. In fact, the computer's fantastic speed in mathematical logic and feedback will increase the capacity of the human brain in a manner similar to that in which mechanical transportation has improved human mobility.

Nature communicates through "perception," that is, not via one of the senses and the brain, as when we read or listen, but directly into the whole receptive mechanism of the plant or animal. Our experience of a summer night when the fragrance of plants and flowers combines with temperature and humidity, the croaking of frogs, and the view of trees and sky as we see them in the light of darkness, is perception. Perception is also our sudden and instantaneous awareness of the presence of danger.

We do not dream in words or ideas. We dream in visual images, feelings, or total concepts which combine in the brain in fractions of seconds. Memory uses a similar process when not forced to perform logically. To express a dream accurately in words is practically impossible. The concepts and perceptions which the brain handles in infinitesimal amounts of time mix readily with actual experiences, the result of direct communication with nature, both inside and outside the body, and with the earth and the universe around us.

Man communicates best when "perception" and "intellectual" communication are applied simultaneously. A combination of perception and intellectual communication is, for instance, to apprehend the eyes and facial expressions of the person we are talking to, together with his ideas expressed in words.

Until not long ago, perception of things and events could be achieved only by personal experience and could be stored only in the memory. Artists interpreted human perceptions and made them available to man through time and space. On the other hand, this was a subjective interpretation, often very rich, but not accurate. There was no substitute for having been there so far as accuracy of perception of things, places, or events was concerned. "Intellectual" communication material has always had the advantage of being storable without loss of accuracy and has made possible the transfer of ideas in time and space. Aristotle's thinking was man's great treasure during the Middle Ages. Goethe's writings were read all over the world in his time and are available to us today exactly as they were written. The first step in "intellectual" communication was language. The second was writing, which made possible the recording and storage of ideas. The third was printing, which made ideas available to many people. It is difficult to say whether the Renaissance brought about printing or printing brought about the Renaissance. The least that can be said is that without printing the spread of the Renaissance would have taken many centuries. First Poland and Germany, and then the rest of Europe, were printing books and stimulating minds by the end of the fifteenth century. With printing, the Middle Ages might never have occurred.

From the beginning of history, man tried to find ways of making both the perceptive and the intellectual content of an experience transferable simultaneously. For this purpose he engraved words on statues and illustrated writings. Woodcuts were in fact the ancestors of printing and from the beginning, writings were accompanied by graphic illustrations. Engraving was invented soon afterward. As the printing of words improved, so did the printing of images.

With the industrial age, paper became probably the least expensive industrial product. Contemporary systems of communication and high-speed presses, together with transportation, made possible the printing and distribution of gigantic amounts of news and information at very low cost in newspapers, magazines, books, and other printed matter delivered where people live or work. Publications in which color photography combines with printed words convey ideas and communicate the semblance of objects or people for the enlightenment, entertainment, and information of millions all over the world. We owe our advanced system of printing and distributing ideas and pictures to the high level of progress man has reached; and we owe the high level of progress man has reached to the advanced systems of printing and distributing ideas. They have multiplied our experiences astronomically.

In a rather inconspicuous way, cinematography made its entrance with the twentieth century. Primitive sequential placing of projected photographs created the illusion of movement. Captions explained situations or simulated dialogue. Soon, cinematography added sound and color, and for the first time in history man experienced accurate perception of visual images simultaneously with ideas expressed in words; that is, perception and intellectual communication reproduced in a sequence of time.

To describe the life of a little boy in a small village of India, for example, would require a great number of pages in written language, and a child, unable to coordinate these ideas or refer them to past experiences, could never grasp their content. Today, looking at the screen, he can see and hear in a few minutes what man was never able to communicate before and his little body vibrates with more intensity than if he had been there, for the presentation has been organized, simplified, and reinforced with music.

It is no longer necessary to go to the Assembly to hear Pericles or his contemporary counterpart; the drama no longer takes place exclusively in the crowded theaters of Paris, London, or New York. The drama today is attended in empty studios by electronic eyes through which we all see.

In our day, television, through its enormous power of distribution, is doing for cinematography, what transportation and telecommunication did for printing. For a few years, television will continue to be expensive to produce and broadcast, and will cater to the entertainment of the mass low-brow audience, just as early printing did. Eventually it will become less the exclusive province of the commercial world, and, like books and radio today, will provide an ample selection of programs from the most popular to the most sophisticated. Some people complain about television's ephemeral quality. Magazines are also ephemeral. Very few of the millions of books written survive a century or even a decade. Some paintings have survived for many centuries but very few of them have any power of communication left; most of them are simply collector's items. Exceptional programs will survive on tape. If they don't, it will be because they are not needed. Relatively few people have read the great literary creations of man: *The Iliad, Don Quixote, Faust, Ulysses.* More have probably seen any of the important movies or television programs.

Printing made progress possible at undreamed-of speeds; man and his society have made more progress in the last four hundred years than in the previous 100,000. The communication of perceptions through audio-visual media will do more for man in the next fifty years than printing did in four hundred. From being practically nonexistent, accurate perception material not only has become storable, but with television its distribution to the world has become instantaneous. Intellectual communication has profited from the new media also, but has suddenly been left behind: language remains the same primitive sequence of ideas expressed at the speed of the tongue, and thinking remains its intellectual representation, just as it was 5,000 or perhaps 20,000 years ago. As a result, perception has taken the upper hand. Television advertising, which has already influenced every other medium, uses mainly perception. Advertisers communicate messages instantaneously to the whole receptive mechanism of the audience. This enrichment of communication will create a completely new kind of culture and will eventually force the renovation of the system for intellectual communication, consequently reshaping languages and man's thinking process. (The need for new concepts in language is already evident in computer programming.)

Man enters the industrial and scientific age armed with three powerful new tools: atomic energy, the computer, and electronic communications. All-powerful tools are dangerous. The gigantic power of electronic communication through perception, improperly understood or used, could be as destructive to human society as atomic power could.

In the past, men were subjected to perception in a natural way. As with everything in nature, the experience was complete and balanced, and provoked within the individual the corresponding spiritual and intellectual adjustments. If a man perceived danger, his instantaneous reaction was to defend himself or run away. If he perceived cruelty, his whole mechanism reacted toward action. When opportunity was in front of him, his intellectual and physical being prepared to take advantage of it, whether it was the ripe fruit hanging from the tree, the cool water to calm his thirst, or the encouraging young female.

Audio-visual communication creates instantaneous reaction, but because the condition of the receiver is passive, his immediate reactions are wasted. The audience becomes accustomed to being passive, to receive, absorb, accept. Here lies the danger of the powerful new media of one-way communication. Books, magazines, newspapers, are also one-way communication, but they are mostly low-power "intellectual" communication. The material has to be digested through thinking—visual images have to be built to simulate reality. In spite of this drawback, publications proved to be very powerful from the beginning. Printing brought about the Reformation, as well as the great physical and social changes of the modern world.

The subconscious manipulation of feelings that movies or TV can achieve with their semihypnotized audience is illus-

Masonry Work in Egypt, Thirteenth Century, B.C. Courtesy of The Metropolitan Museum of Art, Egyptian Expedition, Rogers Fund, 1930.

trated by the international importance movie actors reached in the last four decades and the fame of television personalities today. The popular and sometimes hysterical esteem for an actor over every other personality—political, intellectual, or social—may be stupid but it is harmless; the tremendous popularity of a few mediocre television personalities is of no importance in itself. Yet this adulation demonstrates that with a large enough investment, any person or any group can become loved and admired, the two basic criteria for choosing leaders in a democracy. The world has yet to see the full power of perception communicated with the proper techniques. It is not true that it is impossible to fool everybody. It can be done if "everybody" is taken one by one. Television does just that. Information through perception can very easily become brainwashing.

Until now telecommunication of perceptions has been one-way from a central station. Personal intercommunication has not yet been and perhaps never will be surpassed. If people meet, people talk. If people talk, people think. Man has to communicate with other men in order to organize ideas. Most people are not writers; they have to talk, listen. This is the exercise of the brain that made Athens, Florence, and Paris, and makes New York today. What the city gave people in the past was intercommunication: the interchange of ideas that stimulates thinking, and at the same time uncovers empty areas of the soul, which man feels urged to fill with knowledge; that engenders the appetite to know, to understand, to create. Great cultures are those in which there were large vacuums which stimulated the appetite for knowledge and understanding. Feeding information, even in the language of perception, even in concepts, even of high quality, does not provide the intercommunication epitomized in the Socratic dialogues that Athens made possible.

No wonder that the fantastically concentrated urban hive that is Manhattan, plagued with arteriosclerosis of the streets, emphysema of the air, and infection in all of its liquid humors, so vulnerable that it has been paralyzed three times in one year for more than a day and for different reasons, no wonder this pre-industrial dinosaur still dominates the intellectual, artistic, and economic life of the United States. No wonder it has almost exclusive control of the publication of books and magazines and the programming of television. Manhattan provides intercommunication by the person-to-person system with which man will have to live for some years. Athens and Florence were cities of less than two square miles in which people could walk easily from one place to another, and man could meet man. Although Paris and Manhattan are places of many more inhabitants and many more square miles, people can still meet in them with relative ease.

In the gigantic pan-urban areas of the future, with extensions of thousands of square miles, ultra-fast transportation to facilitate human contact is essential. The creation of any important culture and perhaps even the survival of civilization will depend on the availability of intellectual mating places at the scale of the world, the nation, the region, the urban area, and the neighborhood in which people will be able to exchange person-to-person ideas and experiences. Now that the potential exists for everyone to have a receptor of information at his house, and a fast-moving machine for transportation at his doorstep, people will have a greater opportunity and a wider choice of meeting other men. Under these conditions, chances are that human beings will achieve greater heights of understanding, knowledge, and wisdom.

In the minds of intelligent and well-informed architects of forty years ago, there was no question that the house, a left-over from the agricultural age, was going to suffer a drastic transformation during the industrial era. Le Corbusier, in the twenties, talked about *la machine à vivre* in the same idiom of those who produced flying machines industrially. One of the most surprising phenomena of our time has been not only the survival of the house, but the survival of ancient methods of producing it.

We know how to build machines that fly hundreds of people across the Atlantic faster than sound. We can produce computers capable of one billion operations per second. We can send men to the moon. But we construct houses with the same systems used 300 and even 5,000 years ago. There are some apparent differences—there have to be. There is now a complete range of industrialized products and equipment that go into a dwelling. Some materials are new and industrially produced: plastic tiles for floors, glass fiber for insulation, etc. There are wires and air conditioning equipment that did not exist in past centuries. But the foundations, walls, roof, and floors are very much the same. Wood, brick, and concrete block are so similar to the construction materials of the past that we could take advice on their use from a Greek of the fifth century B.C., a Roman of twenty centuries ago, or a good craftsman of the Middle Ages. None of those people could tell us anything about the modern mechanized farm, cold storage, or canning food. They would be completely at a loss in a factory producing synthetic fabrics or manufacturing clothing, and would be flabbergasted and probably flee in fear from a chemical manufacturing complex, or a factory making sophisticated weapons; they would not believe their eyes at the sight of gigantic earth movers and would think a cyclotron simple insanity, but they would feel very much at home in the construction of a house from two-by-fours or blocks of mud, whether called concrete or brick.

Many efforts have been made to industrialize the construction of houses. Most have been unsuccessful. During World War II, it occurred to more than one airplane manufacturer that his equipment could produce houses that would sell in peacetime in the same volume as airplanes in war. There was investigation and models were built, but nothing was finally produced on any important scale. Companies the size of United States Steel experimented in manufacturing houses during World War II. Thirty years later they are still experimenting. Aluminum companies also experimented. Fiberglas trial models have been built by large chemical manufacturers. Cement companies have produced pilot houses from precast parts or by pouring a whole house on a mold. None ever got very far beyond the picture-taking stage.

The largest and probably the most successful effort has been made in the prefabrication of wood houses. Twenty years ago, there were close to four hundred companies, large and small, producing them in the United States alone. Today fewer than half that number are left, while production has dropped to a dribble. The prefabrication of parts for houses—trusses, windows, doors; panels for walls, ceilings, and floors—has increased. There has also been progress in assembly-line erection of houses. All this has reduced the time and cost of construction by twenty percent to fifty percent. These houses, on the other hand, lack the detail and craftsmanship of individually built structures.

Digging and moving earth is done today entirely by machines better and faster than by hand. There has been a substantial saving in time and labor costs in that type of operation.

Since building man's houses is an international problem involving so many people with such great resources for such a long time, one wonders why this, financially one of the most important industries in the world today, has not been incorporated into the industrial age on any appreciable scale, why it has not demonstrated the same fantastic reduction in price as most products that have improved in quality. One hundred years ago it cost about the same and took as long to make a 3,000-mile trip as to build a house. Today, as we all know, proportions have changed a little, not only in cost, but in time. Today in the United States, a garage made of simple pieces of lumber or any other construction material costs as much as the automobile that it is to house, although a standard automobile has approximately 5,000 different parts made from forty kinds of materials, highly tooled and precisely put together.

The construction of large buildings has been industrialized and mechanized on a larger scale than the construction of the individual house. Nevertheless, the cost per dwelling unit today is not less in an apartment than in a house. The large structures do at least have potential for industrialization since people do not seem to object to apartments or offices exactly the same as their neighbors'. Nobody seems to like the idea of a house exactly the same as his neighbor's, and much less like that of one hundred other neighbors. On the other hand, modern industry is based on mass production of standardized articles for mass consumption. Perhaps the insurmountable obstacle to the introduction of the house into the industrial age has been that it is intrinsically a hand product; in other words, it is like trying to mechanize walking or individual handwriting.

It was logical that people in the past didn't like the idea of a horse carriage exactly the same as another man's; it wouldn't have made sense because both were made by hand. In fact, to make two identical ones would have been a very difficult requirement to impose on a craftsman. But very few people object today to sitting in identical chairs with three hundred other people in an airplane identical to hundreds of others. Perhaps the solution will come the day that people are offered dwellings with all the comforts and gadgets that contemporary science and industry can produce, and at the price of a 3,000-mile trip or even a 30,000-mile trip. On that day, chances are that people will accept many things that seem rather unacceptable today.

Standardization is not the main roadblock. People lived in standardized dwellings for many years; in fact, from the beginning of civilization until less than two hundred years ago. Not only Indian tents and African huts, but houses all over the world were built from a few models, repeated generation after generation. The Cape Cod cottage is a model with fewer basic variations than the present automobile. In urban houses standardization of models has existed to an even greater extent. The Roman house, the Spanish house, and the brownstone house are standard. The Spanish colonizers built only four or five models from Mexico to Chile, from the hot, humid valleys to the cold mountain plateau. They were not identical, since they were handmade, but they shared the same basic characteristics. For thousands of years almost all the important cities of the world were located in the Mediterranean basin. All those cities had standardized types of houses. The house in Aztec Mexico was standardized and so were (and are) most of the houses for each of the regions of China. What is pleasant about the Spanish village or about Paris is a certain "standardization" of buildings. Standardization of houses does not mean standardization of people any more than the fact that all men in the Western world wear trousers and jackets makes them standard. Furthermore, identical dwellings do not necessarily look or feel the same. The apartment of a conservative lawyer does not look at all like the one of the progressive young architect next door, or that of the three teenage girls across the hall.

Attitudes toward standardization are only part of the problem. The main obstacle is the fear which holds people to the agricultural era in which they feel secure, and keeps them from entering the scientific and industrial age in which there are no familiar guidelines. Following traditions has always been simpler than building them. This is not a new attitude. It is rooted in a process which originated in Europe, and especially in England during the nineteenth century, when large numbers of farmers moved to the cities. These country people suffered, but industry paid them well. Soon these farmers, prosperous with industrial money, built farmhouses in the cities. Promoters and developers saw an obvious profit in satisfying peasants' yearnings and diligently built large sections of the cities, especially in England, of "cute" country cottages, one next to the other. When industry later produced larger financial benefits for more people, the new urban bourgeoisie demanded not poor farmers' dreams, but houses for country gentlemen and villas and palaces. The standards for villas and noblemen's palaces have been lowered lately as large masses of them are built in suburbia with standard Federal Housing Authority (FHA) loans and on standard fifty-foot lots.

The individually designed house of wealthy Suburbia, U. S. A., is a copy of the country estate of Europe of the eighteenth and nineteenth centuries, made smaller to survive in a servantless land and age. In some sophisticated cases the houses have been made to resemble not rich, but peasant dwellings. With a flat roof and a few large panes of glass, they have become very popular among the simple, unpretentious, humble, rich, superior intellectuals who enjoy living in the woods.

Noblemen surrounded their palaces or villas with pleasant, ample gardens and terraces beyond which was the open country. In our modern suburbs the gardens and terraces are very small. The "open country" is ten feet wide. In the cities, noblemen's houses had only limited space around them which could not provide enough privacy, so the open space was built within the palace or the mansion. The same was true, in many cases, of the small merchants or craftsmen, or those that were civilized, that is, accustomed to live in cities. The open spaces of the urban houses in Florence or Seville were enclosed and gracefully interwoven with the interior spaces, as has always been true of urban Japan or China. As in a piece of sculpture, it is on this interrelationship of the positive and negative spaces that the architectural quality of the dwelling rests.

Urban houses, properly conceived, can be placed next to one another and still provide the owner with privacy. Rural houses cannot, and when placed side by side, as in modern suburbia, molest, interfere, and clash with one another. The

house becomes a poor "refuge" from friendly neighbors, kids, cars, dogs, and lawnmowers. The natural reaction of the owner is to move farther away. Shrubbery provides some degree of privacy and a mirage of isolation in modern suburbia, as nature in its infinite wealth is generous in camouflaging man's mistakes.

A dwelling of the industrial era that looks and is built like a country house of eighteenth-century agricultural Europe is more than an anachronism; it is a joke. In a few years we will laugh at the houses we build today. They will look as incongruous in a world of space travel and television as a fireplace would in a jet airliner. A contemporary dwelling of the industrial era should, of course, not look like anything done by hand in the past for the same reason that those attractive European country residences of the eighteenth century do not resemble the Indian tent or the Eskimo igloo, typical dwellings of the hunters' era. The industrial dwelling is yet to be conceived and produced. What it will be like is one of the most intriguing questions of our time. Here lies the most profitable industrial frontier.

Why has this riddle which affects the way of living and the economy of the whole world not been solved? For the United States the reasons could be:

(a) Almost all efforts have concentrated on building rural units for urban land.

(b) Most efforts have been addressed to the incongruous production of a handmade object industrially.

(c) Builders, and especially home builders, supply ninety percent of the market with the products of their own ideas. Their ideas are very limited.

(d) Architects have not had the fruitful relationship with industry that engineers have. They are not even involved in the building industry.

(e) Financiers are not interested in seeing the cost of construction reduced to one-half or one-tenth of what it is today, while they hold forty-year mortgages on present buildings.

(f) Labor's medieval attitude toward improved construction methods has helped to keep the industry medieval.

(g) The various and incongruous building codes reflect the primitiveness and parochialism of the industry and simultaneously tend to perpetuate that condition.

(h) The federal government could have given enlightening guidance in land use and construction methods as it has in economic development and public health. But instead of using the leverage of its mortgage insurance to raise the level of the industry, the FHA has been its reactionary business partner. The federal government now makes money on the FHA at the same time that it builds public housing and helps poor people pay the rents that high construction costs and wasteful land use demand. It has, in sum, for many years made possible the perpetuation of ancient, wasteful, inefficient methods by tenderly helping the industry at both ends. It has been only in very recent times that the federal government has understood the need of finding an industrial solution to the housing problem.

The BREAKTHROUGH operation started by HUD in 1969 for

the development of industrial methods of producing housing came forty years too late and out of scale: $15 million for research and development. Simultaneously, the United States budgeted $5 billion for the development and construction of six shuttle vehicles for NASA. The second is not out of proportion; the first is.

It is quite obvious that the residential areas of the future are not going to be clumsy conglomerations of eighteenth-century European mini-mansions sitting on mini-farms. It is also evident that the problems of the American city today are to a great extent the result of the incongruity between this sort of housing and the contemporary industrial and scientific era. Handmade cottages on mini-farms simply do not mix successfully with electronic communications and mechanized transportation, nor do they mix with the present gigantic purchasing power of the people.

Today's house is a handmade piece, an incredible leftover from the past, a relic. As long as it is here, while this situation lasts, a house should, of course, show its handmade quality. Who would like a piece of handworked leather to imitate plastic? But the day will soon come in which custom-made houses will be only for those who can also afford custom-made yachts.

Oone of the most dramatic human achievements of the last century has been in transportation. What makes it dramatic is the speed at which the impact of industrialization changed conditions, making it possible for the present generation to travel, sitting in comfortable lounges, at speeds faster than sound, at the same time that in some parts of the world the burro, the ox, and the camel are the chief and, perhaps, the only means of transportation. Children who watch television today identify equally with the cowboy sitting on the horse and with the spaceman riding a rocket directed by computers.

Transportation at the time of the American Revolution was technically the same as it was 2,000 years before the *Iliad* was written. Then, at the beginning of the nineteenth century in England, the steam engine was invented and applied to the rail-wagons that had been used in the mines for many years. That was in 1814. By 1825 the first railroad was built for public use, and in 1830 came the Liverpool–Manchester Railroad (thirty-five miles per hour). By 1869, the American continent was spanned from coast to coast by railroad.

The steam engine created the first mechanized transportation. Railroads crossed continents and ships traveled between continents. Cities were connected. People and things could be moved easier and faster. Then came the electric motor. The first streetcar operated in Richmond, Virginia, in 1888. Within two years fifty-one American cities had them. The internal

"From the Ox to the Airplane," by Le Corbusier. Courtesy of the Carlos Martinez Collection.

combustion engine, the ancestor of the one used in the automobile, was first made in France in 1860. A more developed
model was built in Germany in 1883, and was soon applied to
a bicycle. The first automobile with a gasoline motor was also
built in France in 1891. The United States built its first automobile in 1892. By 1964, seventy-two years later, there were
81,298,000 in the United States, or an average of one for every
2.3 persons. By 1970, production reached 10 million per year.

Without the iron and steel industries which had developed
in England in the eighteenth and nineteenth centuries, there
would have been no motors or automobiles. Without the idea
of interchangeable parts conceived in France in the eighteenth
century, there could have been no mass production. Without
mass production, cars could not have been made at a price
people could afford. Without mass consumption of cars, the oil
industry, which supplies the gasoline for the fuel and the as-
phalt for the roads, would never have developed, nor could a
network of good roads have been financed and built. Concrete
as a reliable and technically controlled material was developed at the end of the last century. Together with the steel industry, it permitted the construction of bridges, tunnels, and
durable pavements to make land transportation what it is today.

The internal combustion gasoline engine was perfected and
made more powerful and lighter until it could pull an aircraft.
Once a principle is discovered, development comes fast, if a
product is needed and especially if it can be used as a weapon.
Turbines were first used with steam during the nineteenth
century as an efficient way to create electric power. Gasoline
or kerosene turbines to propel airplanes resulted from the
need for faster and more efficient motors to perform at high
altitudes.

The change in the pace of transportation was not an isolated phenomenon. It was part of a gigantic development brought about by using natural sources of energy on a large scale. What was done in the past by animal energy could now be done by steam, gasoline, electricity, or atomic power. Together with the economic techniques of mass production, mass consumption, financing, and distribution, natural energy has changed transportation and deeply affected human society and, of course, the city.

The automobile is not responsible for the condition of the American city. The automobile performs a small task in the contemporary urban complex, product of innumerable new conditions. Some people with simple minds would like to abolish automobiles in the hope that by doing so we could return to the age when they were not needed. Others would like to simplify the problem by concentrating circulation in a few trunk lines (a group not too different from the first). These people believe the solution of transportation to be fast train lines for linear cities, or elevators for very high buildings housing whole metropolises. The fact is that circulation in the large cities of today is a vital, complex function that cannot be solved simply. In the future it will be even more complex. With a growing population that can afford both to own many things (which, of course, take up space) and the luxury of low density and more leisure, the city will cover vast areas that require extensive and complicated systems of internal and external circulation.

As part of that circulation for a long time there will be some type of individual, motorized, enclosed vehicle to carry the two-to-six people corresponding to the human family. Automobiles are, and for a long time will be, best for errands in low density areas and irreplaceable in leisure time. At a cost of one dollar per pound to buy and 14.5 cents per mile to run, automobiles are hard to beat.

There is and will always be a need for collective transportation between important poles within the pan-urban areas and within nations, continents, or planets. Public transportation works best when speed makes possible a high return per transportation hour. One hour at fifty dollars or more can provide very adequate waiting facilities and a comfortable vehicle. One hour at fifty cents cannot, unless the transportation industry is heavily subsidized (five hundred dollars per commuter per year in Boston). Under some special conditions, rail transportation may be advisable as the main urban system (in pre-industrial cities, for instance, such as New York City where one-half of all rail commuting in the United States is done today). It has the disadvantage that interruptions such as strikes and mechanical breakdowns affect large numbers of people and can interfere with the life of the entire city.

When public transportation is planned for low density areas, one vehicle is required to get to the train and another to get from the terminal to one's destination, which is not practical. People avoid public transportation if they can. People (and the more highly developed animals) do not like to be in close proximity to strangers. There seems to be unanimous agreement that public transportation should be improved, mostly in the hope that other drivers will move off the highways.

But automobiles do not have to be the clumsy outsized machines they are today. To use 3500 pounds to carry an average load of 300 pounds is absurd. Cars could be much smaller. A 1000-pound automobile would also be safer, provided all cars were small and similar in weight; it would create less pollution and require less space. In fact, reducing the average American automobile to one half its present size would increase by approximately fifty percent the capacity of highways and parking spaces. The initial saving in this respect alone would probably be close to 100 billion dollars.

Public transportation could then carry these small cars at ultrahigh speed, allowing the passenger to ride in the privacy and convenience of his own vehicle.

In dealing with transportation, there are only two intelligent criteria: first, the perfect solution can be obtained only by abolishing the need for it. Electronic communication is already making much present travel unnecessary. Many of the activities that cause crowding of the highways, such as shopping and entertainment, can be done without leaving one's home or office. In the future, the education of children may also be accomplished to a great extent through television. Thus with transportation, as with biological reproduction, what would seem to be the logical rate of increase does not necessarily hold true.

The second criterion should be: if commuting is unavoidable, make the time used on transportation short and positive: that is, pleasant and useful. Time spent by millions of people crowded into trains or subways, or driving automobiles through large, ugly sections of town twice a day is a shameful waste. Man soon will be living in large pan-urban areas, larger in population and extension than most people realize. The need for transportation that allows better use of the time involved will become more important every day.

Circulation is so vital in highly developed organisms such as mammals that death occurs the moment it stops. Human society is far from demanding such conditions. On the other hand, our human social organization is evolving rapidly, and the more it develops, the more vital healthy circulation will become.

NEEDED: A NEW URBAN STRATEGY

Today world population is approximately seventeen percent urban. By the end of the century, the world will have a population of about six billion people, and sixty percent of them will be living in cities. This means that in fewer than thirty years the earth will have an urban population equal to the total population of today.

There is, in addition, a tendency for urban population to be concentrated in regions, making those areas far more populated than would seem logical to predict. In the United States, this trend, already strong, will increase dramatically in areas such as the Boston to Washington 500-mile stretch, including Providence, New York, Philadelphia, and Baltimore; the 450 miles from Milwaukee to Cleveland, including Chicago, Detroit, and other industrial centers in between; the Pacific 550-mile strip along the coast from San Francisco to San Diego, including Los Angeles; the 400-mile east coast of Florida from Jacksonville to Miami; the north-central Texas area around Dallas and Fort Worth, and three or four other secondary areas. These regions will draw from the rest of the country, forming a new type of decentralized concentration, some of which will reach the hundred millions during the first half of the next century.

Thirty years from now the population of the United States will be about 335 million, or seventy percent larger than it is today, of which three-quarters, or 252 million, will be located in concentrated areas. The territory covered by the urban areas will grow not only because of the increase in population but because of a tendency to decrease in density. Even in highly concentrated areas like New York, population between 1950 and 1960 increased by fifteen percent while the territory covered increased by fifty-one percent.

In those countries that now depend mostly on agriculture and mining, the advent of industrialization, even on a minor scale, will improve conditions so that overcrowding of poor people in small areas will tend to be alleviated. In the industrialized countries production efficiency will increase dramatically through the use of computers and automation. People will have more things and more free time, both of which require more space.

New space requirements will come from the readaptation of the cities to the industrial and scientific era in services and installations. Even the most advanced cities of the world today are still living with the same great discoveries of the last century: water and sewer pipes and telephone and electric wires which make them as up-to-date as the Model T Ford.

It is quite obvious that the problems of the new pan-urban areas are going to be gigantic. It is also quite obvious that these problems cannot be left to the hazard of solving themselves. For if it is true that the future of urban areas will be the result of the conglomeration of innumerable individual decisions of the people, it is also true that trends can be directed toward a common good or can be left to entangle themselves in innumerable conflicts.

The free economy of the United States, as an example, is guided today by brakes, accelerators, controls, and standards of performance, for good beyond the individual's personal interest. Guided regional development could create the proper relationship between built and open land and among the areas where people work, exchange, live, and enjoy their leisure. In the past this relationship was simple: the city, very concentrated, sat in the middle of the open country. People produced in the back of the house, sold in the front, lived on the second floor, and spent their free time in the plaza or the nearby countryside. In many parts of the world they still do. When industry arrived, the city produced in the outskirts, sold on Main Street, and people lived next to both. Fast, inexpensive transportation, immediate long-distance communications, and the scale of human population have changed all this.

Industry was born in cities and for many years stayed there, creating congestion and polluting the air with noise and fumes. Today in the United States, large industry produces on a national and world scale and its location next to where people live is in most cases unjustified. Industry is already moving out to regions where land, power, and water are abundant and inexpensive. Industries are grouping together, since one type of industrial operation usually depends on another. This trend toward the concentration of production will affect large geographical regions. The side effects of congestion and pollution may be disastrous. Not only vast capital investments but human welfare will depend on the right or wrong location and the interrelation of areas where people work, exchange, live, and spend their leisure.

The prospect of vast populations agglutinated in pan-urban regions is frightening. It can generate either catastrophe or a new and better environment for man.

Solutions should be on the same scale as the problems they are to solve. We use massive financing and mechanical equipment to build ports, canals, highways, dams, and rockets; yet the needs of the city are conceived on the financial and tool scale of the wheelbarrow. At the beginning of the century, for example, there were only 250 miles of paved roads in the United States. By 1975, an interstate system of 40,000 to 50,000 miles of four-, six-, and eight-lane super-freeways will be completed at a cost varying from one to three million dollars per mile. These highways are being built by heavy modern equipment, supported by an industrial economy that has more than doubled both gross national product and personal income in the last fifteen years. This is the same kind of industrial economy that made rebuilding possible for Germany and Japan within two decades of their thorough destruction in World War II. It is the same type of economy that made it possible for the United States to throw away two billion dollars a month for several years in a useless and needless war in Vietnam.

It is true that it is always easier to make important decisions and to take important steps under pressure and that there is no greater pressure than the feeling of danger and the instinct of self-defense. The collapse of the economy in the thirties generated the economic planning that made possible the survival of the free enterprise system. Pollution, congestion, and decay have brought urban America to a similar prostration which has already generated its defense reactions. Today the country is in the mood to find within this decade a permanent solution to the urban problem.

In the past, and in some groups at present, there is suspicion about what are called "great schemes." The original settlers' idea was to concentrate on immediate neighborhood problems and to avoid aristocratic, intellectual, and aesthetic preoccupations dealing with generalities which they felt to be the cause of religious and political struggles in Europe. Yet not too many years later the United States came out with one of the greatest schemes the world had known in the Declaration of Independence and in the principles of the Constitution. Nevertheless, it often seems that the interest and dedication of those citizens who could best help in community affairs are dissipated on minor and sometimes insignificant neighborhood problems, while the main issues are left to chance. Many people still believe that working with one's own hands will save the world, that an ocean liner will sail best if everybody, including the captain, works and sweats down in the boiler room.

It is impossible to solve present and future problems with yesterday's concepts. Prejudice confuses thinking. There is, for example, a general prejudice against the large extension of some present American cities when what is objectionable is not their size but the chaos and waste with which the cities are extending. They have to extend to hold the growing population and they can extend because there is instant electronic communication and fast mechanized transportation. And the extension is not really so great: one hundred million people, fifty percent of the nation's population, are concentrated in the 206 urban areas which together occupy an area approximately equivalent to Lake Michigan.

There is a general prejudice against planning, as a curtailment of freedom, when what is wrong is to take planning as an end or as a means to a wrong end. Many feel that planned order is equivalent to regimentation. But in order we find health, and life is based on a continuously changing order. Decay and ugliness are disorder. Death is disorder. The city does not need static order. What it needs is a pattern of development to allow freedom and change within a frame, as grammar gives to language. The frame, like grammar, would also evolve, but if properly devised, it would allow for continuous

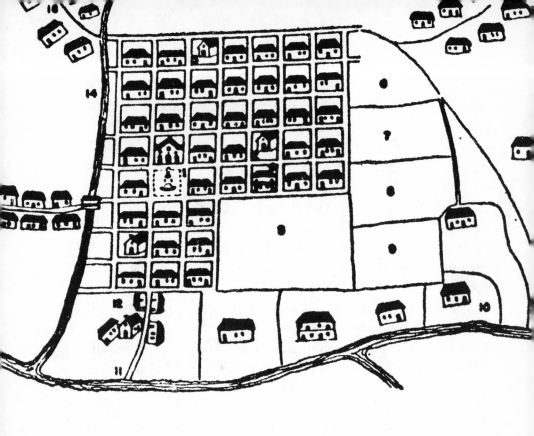

Original plan of the city of Medellin, Colombia. Courtesy of the Carlos Martinez Collection.

change in context while the frame undergoes a slow process of evolution.

Planning cities requires understanding life as the most perfect interrelation of space and time we know. Life, nature, and man are one: no meaningful interpretation of the history of man is possible without understanding life and nature, and no conception of man's future is possible without interpreting nature's past. In the planning of cities time is as important as space.

Time is an element as divisible and plannable as space, but is abstract and therefore difficult to imagine separated from a space container. (In the clock, we measure time with space.) Because of its ability to handle time, the brain has been the successful apparatus it is. Its great role in the development of animals and especially man, has been to provide in new situations judgment based on similar conditions already experienced. Thus the animal able to foresee danger or guess the presence of food in the face of similar but not identical conditions is more intelligent than the one that requires identical circumstances in order to react, and much more intelligent than the one that does not learn and does not anticipate the future.

Primitive societies lack a clear understanding of time. It is difficult for them to plan the strategy that has brought success to more developed cultures. The Roman legion was unbeatable not because of its form but because it used strategy, which is a frame within which a sequence of events happens in time. Its enemies copied the physical formation but could not copy the strategy because they could not think in terms of time. A modern industrial state is a complicated mechanism in which time plays as important a role as space. Its economy is far from that of the simple farmer who thinks in space only and divides his money into piles to be spent on separate things. The difference is the concept of time. Rate of economic growth, rate of expenditure, cost of living, these are all values that, if gauged accurately, would show constantly wavering needles.

Perhaps the greatest flaw of United States policy toward other countries has been its disregard of the fact that the agricultural age did not require elaborate planning in time, dealing as it did with animals and plants that had their own inborn schedules, their own inborn time planning. The people of the United States would themselves in the past have seemed equally unpredictable, irrational, and capricious if judged by the new industrial concept of time-space planning. On the other hand, this basis for judging man and societies may some day turn out to be just as naive as the mechanical concept of life of the eighteenth and nineteenth centuries.

Tomorrow's Urban Shell

People have had visions of dream cities for many centuries. The "city of the future" appears again and again in architectural and popular science magazines. Cities like strange pyramids, conglomerations of castles that lose their pinnacles in the clouds as they reach for heaven. Cities made of enormous craters in the earth, as if for gigantic termites. Towers of colossal playing cards, full of dwelling units. Cities composed of multi-storied floating barges. Cities made of intricate bridges, like lace hanging from the sky, and cities made of a combination of tunnels and towers in fantastic sculptural forms. Cities made of two, three, or four gigantic cubes, cylinders, cones, polyhedrons, or polyhedral groups of polyhedrons, usually placed on gardens. Round cities under plastic domes and cities made of a single long building. Each generation gives its interpretation to the city of the future.

Some, in recent years, have chosen to design the "New City" with a combination of successful architectural elements of present and past; that is, groups of buildings arranged to duplicate successful solutions: the charm of the Piazza di San Marco, combined with Park Avenue, and some small touches of the picturesque narrow curved streets of medieval towns. The Brazilians preferred a modernistic version of the monumental Renaissance city of the nineteenth century, a streamlined Washington, D.C. What these planners—whether from the fourteenth, the nineteenth, or the twentieth century—have in common is their approach to the urban problem from the architectural point of view, the design of cities as if they were gigantic buildings. They are not.

Architecture is the art of organizing materials to create spaces that serve as shelter. In good architecture, inert materials, forms, and spaces are molded into harmony with man. Shelter does not necessarily mean roof, for an open space, whether private or public, can also be a shelter; historically, architecture has included terraces and gardens. The space between buildings, the ground between buildings, and the relations between buildings affect their proportions and are also architecture. For architecture to be in harmony with man, it must be so with a specific man or group of men at a specific time, for men differ and generations change. Architecture is a definite statement in materials, forms, and spaces, and cannot change without losing unity and strength. A masterpiece of architecture is born a finished product. The dimension of time is absent to such an extent that what makes it recognizable as such, is the structure's having frozen the spirit of its time with the materials and techniques of that moment. This is the quality of the Parthenon in Athens, Notre Dame in Paris, and the Seagram Building in New York. And this is the case of the Piazza di San Marco or the gardens of Versailles. All are marvelous conglomerations of materials organized in such a way that the total is a unity not only within itself but with its historical period. And there they stand, fighting time, through generations, as magnificent witnesses of what men did and felt at that moment.

Life is not a finished product. Neither is a city. When a city ceases to have the element of time, of change, it is dead. Equally dead are schemes for future cities that stop time, change, and evolution in men and societies, in order to achieve neat urban solutions. There are many of those, based on what man should want and societies should do, but not only at the moment: man is to continue wanting and societies behaving the same forever.

Some of these schemes are intricate and decorative not only from the graphic but from the social point of view. Few last a year beyond their date of publication. Once in a while one survives a century. Out of Victorian England came one that in spite of, or perhaps because of, its negative approach toward the city, had and still has, acceptance by those who believe in the pastoral nature of man. It is Ebenezer Howard's *Garden Cities of Tomorrow* published in 1898.

Howard was a strange combination of social reformer and astute businessman. During the nineteenth-century industrial development of England, London drew large numbers of poor workmen from the farms. Since it was economically impossible to improve housing conditions and reduce density in the slums, because concentration had increased land prices enormously, Howard invented the scheme of buying inexpensive land in the countryside and building cities surrounded by farms, where people could live and work in idyllic conditions forever. This concept of the contact of farmers and industrial workers was important to him and to a nineteenth-century Victorian England which thought farmers clean and good and city people dirty and full of sin and gin. This romantic idea has not died. Even today garden cities are built in England, the Scandinavian countries, and the United States. Some of them are simply bedroom suburbs, planned to keep some things out, like billboards, and a few things in, like good architecture and pleasant landscaping. Others are more serious in their approach. Developers try to make them into villages where people live and work. These are the so-called satellite cities: fake villages, modern Williamsburgs, romantic illusions, paranoid escapes from reality. Here man, after so many years of striving to enlarge his opportunities and widen his freedom of choice, of work, of friends, of entertainment, finds that there is very little choice.

Industry has changed a great deal since Howard saw it at the end of the last century. A single industry today occupies more ground than Howard thought a future city would.

The back-to-the-womb approach in the design of cities is not exclusive with Howard. Some planners have compared the chaotic conditions of the American city today with successful cities of the past and have proposed copying what others built for other people at another time. They see the deterioration of the downtown areas in most of the large cities of the United States and react emotionally toward nostalgic remembrance of the busy, charming plazas and sidewalk cafes they saw in Europe, which were supposed to have appeared in America by now, and never did. The reaction is to build them immediately and artificially, in an attempt to re-create what made some cities of Europe culturally important. They feel that all efforts should concentrate on the reconstruction of the decaying core of the American city, in a contemporary architectural idiom, perhaps, but following the patterns of the best European examples. They fear the complete collapse of the country's civilization unless the center city is rebuilt; logically enough, since they believe the city's heart and brain are vanishing. What they do not realize is that most of the functions of the urban core have been decentralized or taken over by a communications complex distributed throughout the nation.

Some other planners, seduced by their own nostalgia, have convinced themselves that there are really no problems in the contemporary American city, except those man is creating with bulldozers, steel, and concrete in his urge to solve imaginary ills. They believe that the industrial and scientific age, the colossal population and economic growth of the urban areas, the evolution of the cities from places of residence to producing giants is not very important. They think that the impact of the new means of transportation, the movement of population toward the suburbs, and the people's attitude toward separation of land use are all nonsense. They feel there is nothing like the cozy old sidewalks of the immigrant sections of Boston or New York, and that all efforts should be channeled toward maintaining and creating similar neighborly conditions in the cities.

With the federal government offering financial assistance through a variety of well intentioned, improvised legislation, which the Department of Housing and Urban Development is trying to put together into a workable program, a new kind of so-called "planner" has made his appearance. These planners approach cities, counties, and states offering their services as experts in securing financial assistance from Washington. Since knowledge of the mechanics of the programs, the filling of forms, and the preparation of long reports has become a science, the planners guide their clients into unnecessary and often irresponsible projects, successful only from the point of view of impeccably handled red tape.

But perhaps the most harmful performance comes from those city planning firms with no particular ideas—big corporations which make very important studies for very important sums of money, investigations so complete that there is no time or space for solutions. The problems approached from the sociological, ecological, geological, and ten more "logicals" require hundreds of investigations and thousands of statistics. They produce innumerable facts in huge reports with hundreds of graphs, diagrams, and maps, all extremely interesting and essential but nobody knows what for.

Since these firms have many divisions and many salesmen and public relations men, their presentations are indeed impressive, especially at civic meetings where they summarize their conclusions in what some people want them to say: nothing. This leaves the field open for small politicians and big contractors to recklessly create gigantic projects that will become the gigantic problems of tomorrow. Then the investigations, statistics, and facts are used in the most politically expedient way to prove that whatever was done was right. These firms work extremely well in acquiring government contracts, propelled by the inertia system, which brings new jobs in direct proportion to the amount of work a firm already has.

The serious planners who undertake studies in depth require in most cases so much time before they can give answers to specific questions that when the study is finished the patient has already contracted several other diseases and the investigation must start all over again. Some cities have been undergoing study after study for years.

Politicians do not like to wait for investigations and reports which do not generate votes. They are under pressure for action both because the city's problems are acute and because changes in zoning affect property values and people's investments. Decisions must be made quickly if the city is not to be paralyzed. Consequently, many important decisions are improvised by engineers, executives in government, and the building industry, who plan freeways and public transportation and make decisions on land use and services.

Engineering is a profession that prepares individuals for handling things and energy, not people. Engineers are competent in mining, production of automobiles, planning refrigeration or irrigation, and in handling materials and equipment for the erection of buildings or bridges. To them efficiency is an end in itself. Engineers' training does not include handling man. The better functioning of man has been and should always be left to physicians, educators, architects, planners, philosophers, and politicians.

Urban solutions proposed by engineers are "technical," that is, directed toward eliminating specific pains. If what hurts is circulation, the solution is freeways. If what hurts is slums, the remedy is slum clearance. If density is too high, more services. Medicine was once at a similarly primitive level of development, and when a man complained of headaches, treatment was applied to the head.

Some of today's engineers are not armed with simple slide rules; the computer is their weapon. Sometimes, to attack urban problems of great magnitude, they group in legions and try to understand everything by means of what they call systems analysis. This approach, successful when applied to specifics, is always misleading for general concepts. It is difficult to predict the future. Few predictions are accurate, and those only in general terms. Detail, when predicted, is always wrong. Technical information, like the instruments of an air-

Preliminary layout for midtown interchange, Miami, Florida. Courtesy of the State Department of Transportation, Tallahassee, Florida.

craft, can enlighten the pilot about the best course to follow to reach a certain point but must never be allowed to determine that point.

When general direction in government and industry is left to engineering-minded people, the result is calamity: freeways for automobiles, automobile taxes for road construction, and more roads for automobiles. The faster and smoother this kind of economic wheel turns, the happier these people are. They like the idea of a country operating like a big machine comprised of many wheels: to them the epitome of a really modern and efficient nation. Sometimes it seems as if the American cities were such machines: taxes produce money for projects in the hope that the projects will generate taxes that, etc.

It is absurd for cities or the federal government to invest large sums of the taxpayers' money on freeways, bridges, sewers, or other important works without a clear idea of their positive or negative impact on the total urban complex and ultimately on men. It is absurd also not to know whether such important investments will be part of the services and installations of the urban areas of the future, for otherwise the investments will not only be a waste but a double waste, since they will have to be removed and replaced. Every important city in the United States today has urgent and mounting problems. Most cities also have the will to undertake the solutions of those problems. Convincing people that something should be done to improve the present urban shell is not the issue—they are convinced. Nor is the issue to move local or national government toward awareness of the urban crisis and the need for urgent action. They may not be aware of the scale but they are ready. Politicians and city leaders may not know the cure, but they know where it hurts. The problem is what to do, in which direction to move.

AN URBAN SOLUTION:
THE PAN-URBAN LAND USE SYSTEM

To judge the merits of any solution for American urban areas, it seems essential to define some specifications. The following—implicit in much that I have said earlier—are suggested:

a) The plan should interpret, clarify, and express what people want as shown by their present and foreseeable patterns of behavior.

b) It must allow freedom of choice, bringing order but not regimentation.

c) It must be an urban solution in space, but also in time.

d) It must make growth of the urban areas controllable in quantity and quality.

e) It must be adaptable to existing urban patterns so that cities can apply it without interference to their normal functioning, and in the amount and at the speed proportionate to their needs and means.

f) Benefits should be felt from the beginning, even when started in a modest and limited way.

g) It must be flexible to allow growth and evolution. It should permit expansion and changes in quantity and quality of land use, installations, and circulation.

h) Its development should lend itself to the best exercise of the free enterprise economic system.

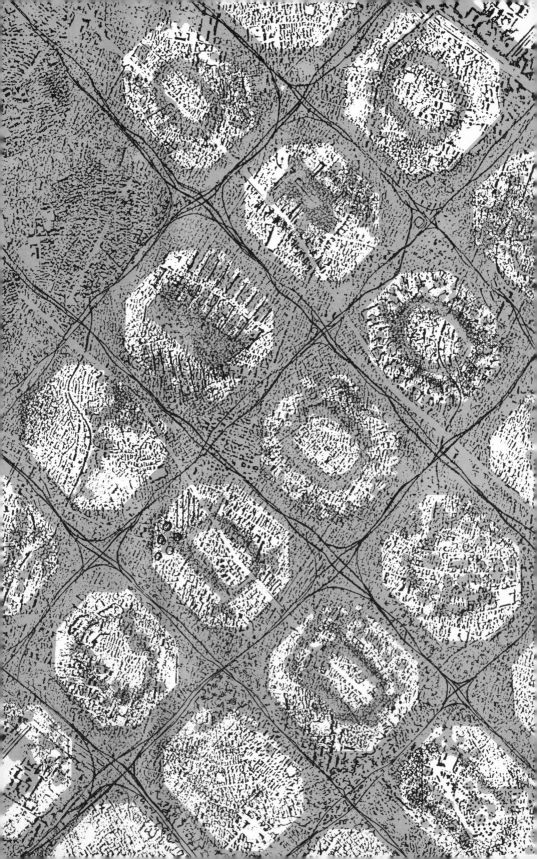

i) It should be a positive tool for the control of the causes of blight and deterioration.

j) It should stop the spread of decay from one area to another.

k) It should stimulate the rebuilding of present derelict areas and slums.

l) It should clarify and simplify zoning by making natural barriers the demarcations of land use.

m) It must allow easy installation and maintenance of the ever-growing system of underground cables, pipes, ducts, tunnels, etc. for communication, transportation, and services. It should make possible the amplification or replacement of such systems, whose complexity will increase enormously in the future.

n) It should make it easy and pleasant for people to get together from distant points of the urban conglomerate; it should encourage personal intercommunication.

The Pan-urban Land Use System *(PLUS)*, the urban solution which I am proposing, meets these specifications. *PLUS* is based on the recognition that the industrial and scientific era is here to stay, that the cities of the agricultural era will have to adapt to it. The sooner they do so, the lesser the evils of the transitional period. The step is gigantic but so are the means available.

Today cities are an amorphous mass of gridiron tissue which proliferate and expand promiscuously, destroying the surrounding landscape while leaving large internal areas of deterioration. *PLUS* replaces this with a system of Urban Units integrated with open land, making possible and practical the control of urban growth in both quantity and quality. The Urban Units are sectors of approximately two square miles of homogeneous character such as residential subdivisions, business and finance, universities, health centers, government complexes, manufacturing or service areas. Separating the Urban Units from one another are the Green Channels, the inter-urban landscape, open land from eighteen hundred feet to one-half mile wide where the main lines of transportation, communications, and services are inconspicuously laid.

Two square miles was approximately the size of the city of Athens of the Golden Century and of Florence at the time of Lorenzo de' Medici. Today, approximately two square miles corresponds to the average residential neighborhood, would contain the financial area of New York, the business center of Atlanta or Los Angeles, the campus of the University of California in Berkeley, or the government center of Washington, D.C. Two square miles means a fifteen-minute walk from the farthest point to the center. The Urban Unit is on the scale of man. The Green Channels, the inter-urban open land, are on the scale of woods, lakes, hills, and clouds. They provide the setting to look at and to look from. There, following the vertical and horizontal lines of the landscape, inconspicuously immersed in ravines covered with vegetation, surface vehicles move at high speed while underground tunnels, ducts, pipes, and service lines have space and are accessible so that they can provide for the present and future needs of the pan-urban areas of the industrial and scientific age.

When the city needs to grow, it creates a new Urban Unit, like a plant producing a new leaf. Growth becomes a clean, healthy, organic process. Uncontrollable promiscuous spread is gone forever. The Pan-urban Land Use System, *PLUS*, is not a plan; it is a way in which urban areas should be organized so that they can be planned. It is a strategy by which present cities, shells of the agricultural era, can be adapted, and saved from the traumatic experience of death before rebirth. By giving the urban areas a more developed organization, *PLUS* can restore health and make future adaptations possible.

PLUS is not a dream. It is a sizable investment; but to continue patching what does not work, and what is falling apart is a useless waste of time and money. Eventually *PLUS* or a similar concept will have to be applied to American urban areas. By then the process of deterioration will have drained much of the strength of the country and the price will be many times higher. Today the transformation of a city such as Boston or Detroit to the *PLUS* concept would cost about two billion dollars, or approximately twice the cost of developing a new bomber. With an average of ten years to transform each city, ten billions in the yearly budget would transform ninety percent of the urban areas of the nation in a period of twenty years. We all know that we can afford it.

PLUS, the Urban Counterpoint

When a man is at rest, when he is asleep, he needs only three feet by seven feet. When he is awake, and at home, he needs a room, perhaps several rooms. This has not changed basically in 500 years, or even 5,000 years.

Outside he walks. He likes to walk as long as he is in pleasant surroundings. No hurry, exciting things to see. Store windows, other people, the sky, trees. He can sit down, enjoy the sun, enjoy the shade, enjoy conversation with others, enjoy birds, plants, water. When cities were small, these pleasures were available to everybody. The task of urban planning is to restore what is worth keeping, and to create what is worth having.

Cities today are very large, because the population is very large, and because we have made a chief out of everybody. The Indians are the machines. We have chiefs and Indians and not just a few but a hundred times the number that could possibly enjoy the space for which the present cities were originally intended. We are all crowding, pushing, and swearing. The solution of sleeping out of the city under the trees was fine until everybody came and put his car under the trees, and soon it was all paved where grass used to be. Moving farther and farther solves the problem of sleeping under the trees, but uses too much time on long unpleasant daily traveling.

The problem of moving ourselves comfortably and safely at high speed is already solved; there are machines that move people and things fast. People like to move at high speed; they hate to move slowly in machines that can go fast. People do not like to push or be pushed and do not like to hurt others or be hurt by fast-moving machines. People like their machines and want to have enough space for those machines to move fast and safely. To walk from the outskirts of Florence to the center of town took Dante or Cellini fifteen minutes. Today riding in machines we can cross in that length of time ten or fifteen *PLUS* Urban Units, that is, twice the width of Miami or metropolitan Washington, D.C.

People enjoy having a pleasant view from the automobile, bus, or train, and do not like looking at junk, whether buildings, signs, telephone poles, or trash. People prefer traveling on well-landscaped parkways today, and are ready to pay for it. They would like to have the main thoroughfares of their urban region landscaped, too. The city can be exciting to look at, an exciting place to look from. People would like to look out the windows of their homes at sky and the green of trees and grass. They would like to gaze across the open land of the Green Channels and see the skylines of other urban units in the bleaching sun or the soft cold mist; or at dusk when two kinds of light talk to one another and the inside light receives from the outside light the mission of keeping the city alive; or at night when the subconscious of the city appears in its garish, primitive, and fantastic neon lights and yellow rectangles.

The big city needs space for everybody, the rich and the poor, the child and the enlightened adult. And the space is there. Most of the space of the present American city is wasted, and could be put to good use. Most cities today could be transformed by the *PLUS* concept without covering more land. Los Angeles and Boston are thirty and twenty percent larger, respectively, than they would be if made into *PLUS* cities. Extension in itself is not bad. Waste is. We need a city for man to walk and children to play in, a city on the scale of man. We have to make the city also on the scale of our fast-moving machines. It is a matter of discrimination of space. Space for people should be at the scale of man multiplied by his speed. Space for fast-moving machines should be on the scale of the machine multiplied by its speed. In the present city, all scales are scrambled. Waiting rooms at docks or corridors in airports are on the scale of man. The ocean liner needs the open sea, the airplane the air, and land machines need land space to perform. Today we have automobiles, buses, trains. Tomorrow there will be other fast-moving vehicles. Surface and underground transportation machines can move fast and need space to move in. They are tools for man, machines to give man more freedom, more choice, more chance. We need areas on the scale of man and to be used by man only—no horses inside the house. Stables for automobiles downstairs. For the dense core of the city it is possible to plan complete separation at different levels. In residential areas separation could be horizontal so that children and vehicles do not go in the same paths.

The small cities of the past were surrounded by open land, where it was possible for children to spend their free time fishing, swimming in the river or lake, and collecting frogs or beatles in the woods. In the large cities today the open country is miles away. In the pan-urban regions of the future, it may be hundreds of miles away. The pan-urban regions will have to provide their own open country for people's use. Public open land should be conceived as national, regional, neighborhood, and local. Each has its own function in space and time. The large national park, for visits during vacations, comprises a geographical region and may be hundreds of miles away. The regional park, for enjoyment of woods, sea, lakes, or mountains during weekends, should be no more than a hundred miles away. The neighborhood park, for picnics and recreation, should interweave with the space where people live and work.

Our concept of tools with which to build and maintain open, landscaped areas is outdated. We think in terms of parks tended by gardeners when they could be maintained the way parkways are, by large motorized mechanical equipment that works better and more efficiently in large continuous areas. Our landscaped open areas could be a thousand times larger with proportionately the same cost and effort as the small town of a hundred years ago spent on its village common.

The agricultural city, concentrated, sitting in the middle of the land, is a relic of the past. That type of urban shell came as a result of other needs at other times. For some regions of the United States, the concept of urban as opposed to rural is already disappearing. This is a tragedy today; it could be the good fortune of tomorrow. In *PLUS*, urban and rural inter-weave, creating an intimate relationship of the urban shell with nature. Many cities of the past are beautiful, not because of their buildings or open spaces, but because of the relation-ship of buildings with open spaces.

The interrelation of built and not built, of positive and neg-ative spaces created by *PLUS*, becomes the new urban counter-point.

It is in this three-dimensional relationship that the city finds its excellence. Like the cathedral of Notre Dame, the Piazza di San Marco, or Henry Moore's sculpture, its value rests on the relationship between positive and negative spaces, the material forms and the spaces they hold.

Since a man moves in and out of structures, the architectural quality of the city depends not only on how the buildings look, or how the city looks from buildings, but on the time integra-tion of both.

The Cloister Park

The Cloister Park is one possible solution for the remodeling, or development of Urban Units. It is based on the belief that people should also be able to be near limited green areas where they can walk, ride bicycles, sit in the shade of trees, and meet other people. These areas, whether conceived as the Roman Forum, the Spanish plaza, or the mall of the modern shopping center, are important and will be even more impor-tant in the cities of the future. The Cloister Park is not a plaza, not a boulevard, not a mall. It is a cloister of green in the core of the Urban Unit. People can move along its sides uninter-ruptedly and so can the maintenance crews with their ma-chines. It serves a maximum number of people in a maximum number of ways with a minimum area.

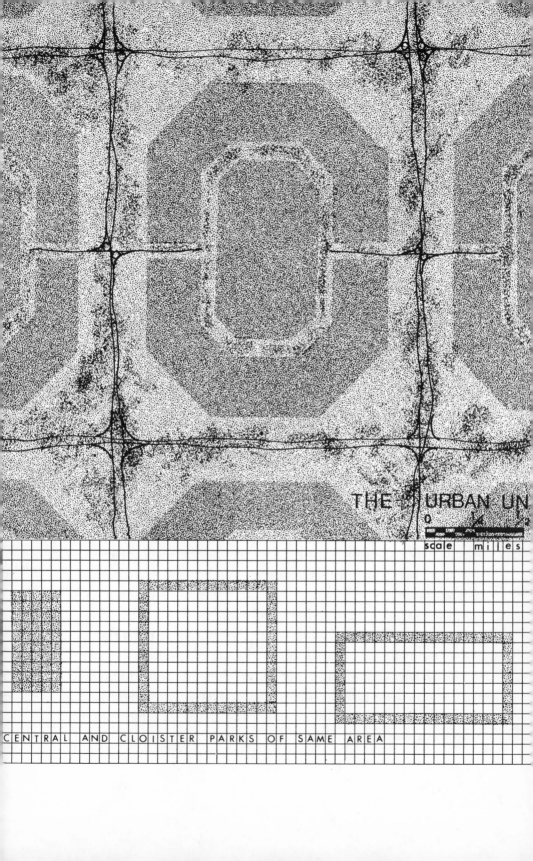

THE URBAN UN
0 ¼ ½

CENTRAL AND CLOISTER PARKS OF SAME AREA

A central park, for instance, five blocks wide by ten blocks long has an area of fifty square blocks with only thirty city blocks adjoining it. A Cloister Park of the same area, but only one block wide, would face and enhance ninety-six neighboring blocks, that is, more than three times as many, and at the same time serve as an attractive zoning barrier. In residential areas it will be possible to walk or ride a bicycle all around the park, surrounded by green, without crossing streets.

In some cases where high density is needed, the Urban Unit may be a platform on which the Cloister Park becomes a promenade with planted areas. Large openings can bring light and air to the lower levels in which vehicles circulate freely. At even lower levels there can be parking, also subways, trains, buses, and other means of transportation. There will be docks for cargo, centers of collection and distribution, storage tanks, and the enormous and complicated internal organs of the great mechanical and electro-chemical complex which some Urban Units will require.

How PLUS Works

The Urban Unit is on the scale of man. Two square miles corresponds roughly to the average homogeneous residential area. It is the minimum that can support civic and commercial facilities in suburbs and the maximum that the average person can grasp in his concept of neighborhood. Two square miles is large enough to permit the exercise of free enterprise without compromising the future of the total. The future of the city is the sum of decisions by many different people, but these decisions must be guided by general concepts. This is the way a modern democracy works and the way democracy can attain high efficiency.

The free enterprise economic system is pragmatic and often short-sighted. It works best in the present and for the solution of immediate problems. The unbridled exercise of free enterprise by promoters and speculators looking for fast profits brought about the financial collapse of the thirties. The reckless exercise of free enterprise in land and buildings has been an important factor in the collapse of the American city, and has failed to generate its recuperation.

The industrialized economy of the United States has conditioned people to the idea that what is old and used should be thrown away and replaced. This gospel of the industrial age is good and true, except when one of the elements is land, which is irreplaceable, and another is buildings, which are difficult to move or throw away. So instead people move away to rural land and abandon the old and used parts of the city. The rapid and irresponsible transformation of rural land into urban property creates fast profits for a few and bankruptcy for the city. In the modern guided economy of the United States, banks and insurance companies are not allowed to expand for the benefit of a few, without meeting standards that guarantee the public's investment. Because of the scattered, chaotic way in which cities now expand, it is impossible to enforce controls.

In *PLUS*, expansion becomes an organic process. When the pan-urban area needs to grow it creates a new Urban Unit. The birth of a new Urban Unit means an important investment of human and physical resources of the entire urban complex. It is only logical that all benefits of land valuation should go back to the conglomeration of humans who made it all possible. That means the entire urban entity. It is theirs. In the *PLUS* city the selfish spread promoter and the land pusher are out of business. In agricultural cities of

the past, extension was controlled by strong centripetal force. Because of limited extension, the price of land was high and its reuse profitable. A similar phenomenon exists today in Manhattan and parts of San Francisco in which expansion is limited by water. Because the PLUS Urban Unit also has limited extension, the demand for land will maintain prices at a level which induces rehabilitation and rebuilding.

At present, decay of one area rapidly spreads to another. In cities that adopt PLUS, contamination will be limited by the Green Channels. Deterioration of the urban tissue is contained. If the Urban Unit is of the cloister type, deterioration is contained within an even smaller area. When decay is checked and kept within limits, stimulation of land values is possible and rehabilitation practical through urban renewal programs or any other system. Under present urban conditions, local remedies are useless.

Fighting the decadence of the obsolete agricultural city with zoning alone is like using buckets to catch dripping water in a house in which the roof is collapsing. Zoning can work as a guide, never as a deterrent. Zoning may improve a healthy shell, but cannot remove the causes or control the spread of urban deterioration. When the agricultural cities were healthy, they were so without zoning. Zoning has not made them any healthier now that they are in the process of decay. As with controls in a deteriorating economy or stimulants in the sick body, it is hard sometimes to know whether the sick economy and the ill man would be better off without them. Zoning can destroy free enterprise: it can also be deadly in the hands of free enterprise.

At one time all functions in a city were mixed. Manufacturing, selling, and residence have become separate in a modern city and particularly in the American city. In fact, they have become so separate that the improper contact of one with the other in most cases becomes a deteriorating agent. Improper use of land for commercial activities can produce decay in residential areas, and because of this decay, engender deterioration in the commercial property itself. Today, manufacturing does not mix well with commerce; none is allowed in modern shopping centers. Poor people who had to walk to work used to live next to factories. Nobody with an automobile wants to live next to factories.

These are the real zoning problems that cannot be solved by paper from City Hall. The separation of the commercial from the residential by a street does not work; no merchant wants to have residences across the street and nobody wants to have stores in front of his house. To separate commercial from residential in the middle of the block does not work. No one wants to look at the rear of stores from his back yard. It can be said that the separation simply cannot be made successfully, that there will always be problems, and that so long as those problems can be solved only by the sacrifice of one and the profit of another, there will be pressures and corruption at City Hall.

If cities remained stagnant, there would be a chance of eventual stabilization. But most American cities are growing and changing. The kind of city in which we live simply does not work for a mixture of manufacturing, commercial, and residential use. Yet they cannot be separated.

For urban areas adopting the *PLUS* concept, these general problems of zoning are solved. The Green Channels are the natural boundaries. Residential, business, government, medical centers, and universities, can be clearly defined in Urban

Units. And in the *PLUS* city, light industries can be located centrally. There will always be a belt of at least 1,800 feet of landscape around them.

The buildings and architectural features of the urban unit will be subject to natural continuous renewal and adaptation, depending on economic conditions and modes of the time. Urban Units originally used for individual residences, for instance, may be used later for high-rise apartments, neighborhood commerce, a highly complicated scientific center with enormous loads of electricity and other services, or a medical and hospital center which requires special installations. These modifications imply drastic change in sewerage and water lines, electrical and telephone cables, gas, vacuum tubes, and underground circulation. The agricultural cities of today were not planned to accommodate such change.

Manhattan's visceral entanglement of cables, ducts, pipes, tunnels, subways, trains, and shelters, is just a sample of what cities will have tomorrow. Today important buildings utilize ten percent of their floor space for equipment and service installations, not counting entire floors which house the controls. In the future, cities' equipment, installations, and services will require a similar proportion of space. Construction of new lines, or maintenance and expansion of old ones, will require major construction which cannot be done through little manholes. The Green Channels will make this possible. The cloister park will make it easier. Radical changes in service lines will be required when two urban areas touch and begin to merge. In the future, many will. Similarly, large new recreation areas may generate important circulation needs which will also require rapid urban adaptation. It is not only essential to have the space available, but alternative space, and the channels, being parallel to one another, will provide it.

As a city shifts to *PLUS* it can set priorities. People can plan in advance. Financing can be based on known conditions. Future development need not be a large question mark. For example, when freeways are needed they go where they should. No improvisation, no guesswork. This is not true today. Freeways are thrown irresponsibly into cities without a clear understanding of the consequences. They relieve circulation pressure on one side and create congestion on another. They give life to one section of the city, and kill another—all this to be realized only after it happens. People have been very patient while the cities have been slaughtered by road engineers. Freeways now destroy property values because nobody wants to be near ugly, noisy, monumental barriers; but who would object to living on a pleasantly landscaped park?

For some time it will not be necessary to build great super-freeways in all the Green Channels. After all, a good road with intersections every mile and a half is an important improvement. But in five, ten, or twenty years they may be needed. What a pleasure it will be to drive by woods, grass, and water instead of the chaotic mess of cheap buildings and parking lots of the present city. It is the same space used more intelligently. And to maintain these beautiful parks will cost less than the upkeep of present derelict areas.

In the Green Channels roads wind through the landscape, creating an infinite variety of vistas. But the Green Channels follow a pattern of coordinates to make orientation simple.

Most medieval cities were overgrown villages. As the points of interest changed through history, the pattern of streets remained a disorganized mesh. The result was chaos. The acceptance of the Roman gridiron pattern of streets and blocks was a great improvement for its time. It brought order and a simple means of orientation. It had the scale of the small, concentrated agricultural city and of one- and two-story buildings. It provided straight lines for drains, water pipes, and, eventually, electricity. In the present large metropolis, however, it has lost its scale and its function and has become unbearable in its monotony.

The New Cultural Nucleus

The great pan-urban areas of the future will need a simple pattern for orientation. The detail can be a mosaic of variety but it is essential to facilitate the immediate physical and psychological location of any point if the city is to regain its function, which is for people to come together. In cities of the past, people met easily by walking either to the central civic places or to one another's shops and homes. In pan-urban areas today, people cannot meet. Distances are too great, traffic too difficult, and public spaces inadequate to contain the crowds, much less their transportation machines. Downtown areas are being abandoned by people tired of waiting in traffic and being pushed by strangers. Centralization of commercial facilities belongs to the past. The scattered shopping centers of today fill the need better. Administrative and financial facilities are rapidly decentralizing. Entertainment is to a large extent replaced by a network of electronic communications spread over the country. Few cities in America have nuclei with important landmarks of the kind European cities built over the centuries. So the core of the city, having lost its function, is rapidly disappearing. There is no need for the core, but people must meet again. *PLUS* will make this possible. Ample channels for high-speed transportation and simple patterns of orientation will make it easy and pleasant for people to go to see one another. The need for people to meet casually for intercommunication still exists. It is essential for urban areas to provide the places in which urban culture is generated through meetings, exhibits, etc. If there are not such centers and people do not meet, the urban area and its people become a mediocre mass, depending intellectually and economically on what is fed to them from other centers in which important intercommunication does exist. Cultural mating places provide the person-to-person intercommunication that television, movies, books, and telephones cannot provide. Intercommunication stimulates the process that makes each individual organize ideas and create concepts, to become an active participant instead of a passive receiver. Person-to-person intercommunication stimulates people to want, creates the appetite for better materials, and impels some individuals to create and contribute to human progress with original ideas. Friends meeting casually around a café table, businessmen having lunch together, comments and criticisms at exhibits, presentations, or lectures, in which people exchange opinions: these are intercommunication.

The political life of a country is created in meetings, and without them it would become a sterile system administering intrigues and funds. Thinking needs stimulation. The American family is becoming a suburban, provincial listener. The concept of the public place where people meet must be preserved, but not the belief that the core of the nineteenth-century agricultural city of Europe is the ultimate shrine of cultural creativity. It belongs to another time, as does the culture it produced. The cultural mating places of the American urban areas have to be created in a new form.

All of the great civic and cultural centers of the past were built by a combination of the ruling powers, mostly state and church. This is true in Europe, Asia, and Pre-Columbian America. During the Renaissance, financial power appeared, and thereafter, during the great splendor of the agricultural and commercial European cities, some magnificent examples were built by a combination of government, church, and financial power. The nuclei of the important European cities were built with the concentrated effort of many people during many centuries, and in some cases correspond to the best product achievable in those times under those circumstances with those means.

The American predominance in the world belongs to the twentieth century. Now is the time for this country to make its historical contribution by creating with its large resources and great energy the physical space in which the man of the end of the twentieth century will flourish.

Today's high level intercommunication in knowledge and science is taking place on the campuses and at industrial and government research centers. There resides the new aristocracy of the mind. There man progresses at high speed while the rest of the people read lowbrow newspapers and watch childish television programs. Those inside are learning while those outside try to forget. Every minute the gap widens. There, on the campus and in those centers, is the seed of great promise but there also could be the beginning of the end of a democracy.

During the Middle Ages the intellectual traditions of Athens, Alexandria, and Rome were kept alive in monasteries and later in universities, but it was only when knowledge came out into the main square that the Renaissance began. Now that commerce no longer belongs in the nuclei, why not create as intellectual and cultural mating places of our urban areas, ample, beautifully landscaped campuses adorned with elegant buildings and pavilions in which everyone could intercommunicate with the pleasure and gusto that people once had in the small Piazza della Signoria? Entertainment does not have to be cheap and in bad taste to be fun. The twentieth century could be brought out of the monasteries for the enjoyment and enlightenment of man. Such a core would not only help the cities but would help man, for whom everything should be conceived in the first place.

At this moment of the urbanization of the earth, we cannot run away from the problem to create nostalgic villages in the countryside, knowing very well that in a few years they will be flooded by amorphous pan-urban development. Nor can we content ourselves with romantic illusions, and reconstruct cities of the past. Such solutions are, at best, pretty stage sets which, even when built of concrete or steel, resist the impact of the new urban evolution no better than cardboard scenery.

The United States is in a position of indisputable economic leadership. Respect and leadership are not attributes of power, but of a combination of power with wisdom. If the United States is able to show the world a way of bringing man to new heights physically, intellectually, and spiritually, it will be the leader and undisputed builder of man's destiny; otherwise, more and more money will be needed to buy friends and destroy enemies.

At this moment of history man is settling permanently in an urban environment. Environment is an ample word which encompasses universal space and light, and also the man-made things which today are replacing the nature-made ones with which life has existed from the beginning. It is up to the present generation to state the lines of that settlement for the scientific and industrial era. For the United States, the most industrialized nation of the world, it is a great responsibility.